A Bit of an All-Rounder

For CYNTH

*Who encouraged me at the beginning of my endeavours
and gave me much valuable support thereafter as my roadside recorder.*

A Bit of an All-Rounder

40 years of cycle photography

John Coulson

A Bit of an All-Rounder
40 years of cycle photography

First published in 2011 by:

Mousehold Press
Victoria Cottage
Constitution Opening
Norwich NR3 4BD

www.mousehold-press.co.uk

ISBN 978 1 874739 60 9

INTRODUCTION

Many years ago when I was a youngish man working for one of Britain's larger finance houses I was transferred to a small office to take the place of a man who was about to retire. On being introduced to this gentleman he looked me up and down quizzically and then remarked, "*You're* a bit of an all-rounder, aren't you!"

This was an assertion rather than a question and I was a little taken aback at first until, on reflection, I took him to mean that I was not in the usual run of stuffed-shirt employees and that it was actually something of a compliment. Looking back at my life from a much later viewpoint his remark had a good deal of unconscious truth in it as I do seem to have employed such talents and abilities as I possess in a wide variety of interests and activities, chief among them being a deep preoccupation with all aspects of the sport and pastime of cycling and, largely arising from this, involvement in freelance photography and journalism.

However, that aspect of my life had not yet come about at the time his relatively unimportant remark was made although, quite fortuitously, it presaged an important turning point. Having spent half a lifetime dabbling in all sorts of activities and enduring twenty years of an unsatisfying job for the sake of security and the prospect of a reasonable pension, I needed something else to give me a fresh purpose in life and provide greater opportunities to do the things I was best at and enjoyed doing most. As indicated, I was a keen club cyclist, having been involved with pretty well every aspect of the sport and pastime but at the juncture of which I write it was becoming quite obvious that any long-held aspirations I might have had in the direction of racing success were so much pie in the sky. Yet I needed something to replace the spur of competition which was on the wane after about twenty years. So I did some deep thinking and came to the conclusion, which I should have reached many years earlier, that one should always capitalise on one's strong points. Thus I asked myself what it was that I did best, and came to the conclusion that the answer was, use a camera and write the English language.

But I am getting ahead of myself. The cycling facet of my life took off in 1945 at the tender age of thirteen when I persuaded my parents to buy me one of the lightweight sports type bicycles then just beginning to reappear on the market after the end of the Second World War. Living as we did in Chingford on the edge of Epping Forest I had a wealth of countryside on the doorstep and I set about a magical exploration of an Essex and Hertfordshire with roads empty of traffic, with petrol rationing still in force, and unsullied by new town developments. Exploring mostly alone at first, I was joined after a couple of years by like-minded schoolfellows. We formed ourselves into a sort of unofficial club for Sunday morning runs and as time went by, for youth hostel weekends to Kent and Surrey and longer tours to the Isle of Wight and the West Country. Youth-hostelling was very cheap in those days and even the last tour, financed by my father, cost no more than £2.50. It had occurred to me during these expeditions that it would be nice to have a camera to take all that wonderful scenery home with me. I had by then acquired quite a collection of books about the English countryside, lavishly illustrated with landscape photographs which I very much admired. However, cameras and film processing were relatively expensive, way beyond my meagre pocket money, and having already coughed up for a bicycle and several youth hostel forays my father could not have been expected to finance me in a photographic venture.

There was much else to occupy me, though. Most of our little 'club' had become avid readers of the cycling journals such as *Cycling, The Bicycle* and the *CTC Gazette* and spent a good deal of time discussing the current racing and our particular heroes as well as the split between the mutually aligned National Cyclists' Union and Road Time Trials Council, and the British League of Racing Cyclists. Leaving that last aside for the moment though, 1948 was the year in which the Olympic Games were revived after the war which gave us the chance to see those big names in the flesh in the road race trials held on our local airfield circuits of Fairlop and Matching Green and finally in the Olympic road race itself in Windsor Great Park. It goes without saying that all of us were involved in some measure in the school curriculum sports of cricket, Rugby football and athletics, but for some of us cycling had taken the premier spot and so inspired were we by seeing all this competition that, largely at my instigation, we ran a short series of races for ourselves – three time trials and a circuit race. These were completely unofficial, no adults were involved, we had no affiliation to any official cycling body and had therefore nothing to fear in the way of sanctions. I venture to say that these were probably the first competitive events ever promoted in Britain *by* schoolboys *for* schoolboys. Certainly they anticipated the formation of the English Schools Cycling Association by something like twenty years.

A completely different facet of my school life was that I found I was quite good at essay-writing, something which was a set weekly task, and I must have written dozens during my school years. Strangely, though, the only ones I recall now were a review of Dodie Smith's play *Dear Octopus*, presented for radio on Saturday Night Theatre, a description of the Battle of Britain as seen from our back garden, and a sort of guide to St Albans which I knew well from my cycling expeditions. For this last piece I remember lifting a short paragraph straight out of a guide book, a piece of plagiarism which was spotted immediately by our English teacher who castigated me for lapsing into 'journalese'! Oddly enough,

although the school had a magazine run entirely by pupils, I never made any contribution to it, considering that doing what was required by the official curriculum was quite enough brain fag.

*   *   *   *   *

Towards the end of 1948 I started work in one of the large banks in the City of London. Not that I had any particular interest in the financial world, I just needed some income to further my interest in the bike game, such as upgrading my equipment and joining a real club. The dissident policies of the BLRC rather appealed to my nonconformist nature and having assembled a machine more suited to my recent growth and requirements I joined a local League club, the East London Racing Club. There I found myself rubbing shoulders with some of the Paris Cycles independent team, Clive Parker, Harry Burvill and Stoppa Clarke, and other amateur stars who would go on to form part of the Hercules professional team, Dennis Talbot and Derek Buttle. I became an habitué of the Alpha and the Angela, those two famous cafés on the Epping New Road and also, a little later, of the equally famous Bomb Hole, with which my illustrations commence.

I was very small fry among all this at first and to be honest it was something of a culture shock for a boy from an over-protected background to find himself among a group whose approach to life was joyfully free-thinking, not to say anarchic. Nevertheless I soon found my feet, developing into the sort of boy my mother wouldn't have liked me to know and launching into a mixture of racing, not with any great success. However I did score a third place in the London Section junior time trial championship, largely because the event took place in a thunderstorm and half the entry retired. In addition, I was very soon introduced to required reading for young Leaguers, the French sporting journals *But et Club* and *Miroir Sprint* whose lavish photographic coverage was a dual inspiration. I also did a tour to the Peak District and North Wales in the spring of 1949 with two old school pals who had also joined the

East London. As it happened, that was the last extended tour I was to do for some considerable time, as will be revealed in due course. Oddly enough, one of those friends was just getting into photography himself and had acquired an Argus, an American model which was the first 35mm camera with which I had any acquaintance. Terms such as cassette were introduced to my vocabulary although at first I had no idea what such an item was. However, my own slim finances at that time could only just sustain my all-pervading cycling activities and I put any nebulous thoughts of photography aside for a later date.

On a completely different tack, at about that time like many young Leaguers I conceived a passion for jazz music and occasionally entertained a fantasy of becoming a jazz musician. This was an obvious non-starter as, although I had learned to play the piano to a fairly elementary level, I could never play a note of any melody without the musical score in front of me: I still cannot, despite having returned to practical music nearly twenty years ago with a domestic organ and, having come to terms with my limitations in that direction, just indulge in it purely for my own amusement.

The great bugbear in the life of many young racing cyclists then was the prospect of National Service looming at the age of eighteen. I knew of several who got out of it on the grounds of conscientious objection but I suspect in most cases it was not so much religious objection, but objection to having their racing careers interrupted. As it turned out, I found my two years in the RAF not unpleasant after initial training was over. The armed forces, the RAF in particular, were keen on participation in any form of sport. As a cyclist I found I could get plenty of time off for training as well as racing in various parts of the country in both civilian and service events, most memorably in inter-service events promoted by Army CU Western Command at Chester where our middling sort of team from RAF Warton found ourselves pitted against some of the best riders in the country. We had little success to shout about but it was nevertheless a great experience. Incidentally, wherever I was during my service time I wrote a letter home every week or two which, although sometimes a bit of a chore if nothing much was happening, it doubtless gave me some good practice for what I am doing at this moment.

Once in the RAF I had little intention of returning to the banking profession. Some of the riders I knew in civvy street were making a career of having a job during the winter to save a packet of cash and then packing up work from about Easter onwards to spend the summer doing nothing but racing and training, and with luck and ability making some return in prizes. Nobody in the sport made any great fortune then, all they wanted was to ride bicycles and pay the rent. In my RAF billet I dreamed dreams of doing that myself after demob, perhaps even making it to the Continent where cycling was a national sport in several countries. However, life always has little surprises up its sleeve and with six months of my service still to run I met the young lady who I knew beyond all doubt was The One!

So, back in civvy street again after my two years was up, I returned to the humdrum round of the city financial world, realising that if my intended and I were to get hitched in anything like the foreseeable future I needed a steady and guaranteed income. Although I continued racing for a time fairly enthusiastically I had noticed with interest the roadside photographers who were around at most events, the likes of Len Thorpe, Ted Lees and the Pegley brothers, offering prints for sale to individual riders and also supplying pictures to the press. Even from my energetic situation on the saddle I noted their Leica cameras and their employment of a 'panning' technique in capturing action. Curiously enough I had come across this much earlier, as a young lad during the war years when I had conceived an interest in motor racing – purely academic as there was nothing of the sort going on at the time – and in one of the library books I perused on the subject there was a reference to the photography of racing cars in motion. One of the problems with early action photos, particularly when using cameras with curtain type focal-plane shutters, was the obvious image distortion which occurred when photographing fast-moving objects such as racing cars, to say nothing of making the exposure at just the right moment. The author of the work, whose name now escapes me, described how he and a few others had developed the art of panning, that is, picking up the subject in the viewfinder as it approaches, swinging the camera smoothly to follow it, pressing the shutter release as it passes the point of focus, and continuing to swing the camera to follow the subject briefly after exposure. All action photographers nowadays use this technique, but when that book was written in the Thirties it was a new departure and although my own venture in that direction lay many years in the future the obvious practicality of it made a lasting impression.

Actually, I did have something of a legacy in photography as my father had been a keen photographer in his younger years, using a Thornton-Pickard reflex, a highly-regarded piece of equipment in the early part of the twentieth century, and doing his own developing and printing from the glass negatives which it used. Indeed he had once won a prize in a competition run by *Amateur Photographer* magazine with a portrait of my mother, yet strangely he had never pursued his obvious talent in that direction and by the time I appeared on the scene in the early Thirties the Thornton-Pickard had disappeared. Thenceforward the only photography I ever saw him doing was to run off the odd roll of film to record the growing-up process of me and my sisters, using cameras borrowed from work colleagues. Those were of the popular inexpensive folding variety then marketed by manufacturers such as Ensign, Coronet and Kodak. I also have a photograph of myself aged about three holding a cheap box camera which my father later insisted was bought for my use but I have no recollection of taking pictures with it and that too had disappeared by the time I have any conscious recollection of my boyhood. So it was many years before I launched into photography myself although I sometimes examined with curiosity the collection of those esoteric-looking negatives which lurked in a drawer in his desk and pondered over the mysterious processes which converted them into pictures with the black-and-white the right way round, as it were.

By the summer of 1953 the racing regime was beginning to pall somewhat. I was introducing Cynthia to my vision of cycling and we were doing some very enjoyable pottering around the countryside. A number of my cycling acquaintances were then taking up photography and I decided it was time I had a camera to record our outings together and depict the attractive scenes around us. I had little enough cash to spare after putting funds aside for our impending marriage, but nevertheless I splashed out somewhere around ten pounds, about a week's money then, for a British-made Kodak folding model. Kodak of course is an old American company but by then had a well-established manufacturing base in Britain as well as in Germany. In fact by then the British camera manufacturing industry was in decline and German manufacturers were dominating the market to an even greater extent than in pre-war years, only to be overtaken by the Japanese in the late Fifties, a supreme irony when one considers they had both supposedly just lost a world war!

Leaving that aside though, I had no truly formulated ideas of what direction I should take with the Kodak; as noted I was particularly interested in landscapes and went around taking a lot of pictures which were actually a waste of time and film and failed to snap a good many things which I should have done. In any case I was a little restricted as, having bought the camera, I was in no position to buy additional equipment to do my own processing. (Actually I did do my first 'freelance' job with this as I took photos of the office football team and sold them copies at a few pence each to cover the cost of film and commercial processing.) However, I had become an enthusiastic reader of *Amateur Photographer* and, apart from picking up plenty of hints and drooling over equipment I could not possibly afford, I noticed a regular advert for Mallinson's School of Freelance Photography and Journalism. I knew nothing at all about freelance employment – my parents would have pooh-poohed it as "not a proper job!" when I was contemplating leaving school – and although I pondered it in an abstract sort of way I did nothing about it as it would in any case have meant more money going out. Very silly of course, as it would have changed my life much sooner than actually came about, but then hindsight is a wonderful luxury.

It soon became obvious that the Kodak had serious limitations for my growing practical interest: its range of shutter speeds was quite inadequate for the action work which now attracted me, and it took only eight exposures per roll of 620 film which made commercial processing rather uneconomic. Thus I spent as much time peering into photographic dealers' windows as I had into those of cycle shops in the years preceding. Eventually I spotted a second-hand Ensign Selfix going for a price which would enable me to make a reasonable part exchange and provide me with a somewhat more versatile camera. Like the Kodak it was a folding model, again British made, but with a wider range of shutter speeds, faster lens and taking sixteen exposures on 120 roll film. The odd thing about these cameras in the light of present-day custom was that they were both made for left-handed shutter release, unheard-of now.

Thus equipped I made my first serious attempts at taking pictures of racing cyclists in action, making my first essays into the technique of panning. This proved much harder than I had anticipated, one tends to panic, swinging the camera jerkily or too fast, pressing the shutter release too soon, or stabbing at it too late: I produced at least one fine shot of the gap between two riders with half a rear wheel at one side and half a front wheel at the other! It was not helpful either that most cameras, other than top grade models, had a rather heavy shutter release, unlike modern products and focussing, too, could be a problem as only the more expensive ranges had coupled rangefinders. Reflex focussing, as incorporated on all modern single lens reflex cameras, was only just beginning to make its presence felt, although the German 35mm Exakta range had been on the market since pre-war years. So it took me some time to get the hang of it, one or two early efforts are included within this volume, and even then it was not until I changed up to a rangefinder camera that I was really happy with results. However, like many other accomplishments, such as riding a bicycle, once mastered

I wondered why I had found panning so difficult and now do it without even thinking about it.

In the meantime Cynth and I had got married and, after a couple of years in which we also took up motor cycling on a very slender budget, I resumed road racing in a desultory fashion. I soon came to the conclusion though that the only way to enjoy the bunched game was to be flying fit and up there with the leaders, otherwise it was a waste of time. As a result I took up time trialling, mostly at club level, which allowed me to enjoy competition without the necessity for too much intensive training

Thus life went on for the next ten years or so, our family increasing, progressing from motor cycle combinations to unreliable second-hand motor cars, my uneventful working life alleviated by a good deal of varied time-trialling. My road racing background led me to a preference for hilly events at odd distances, and as time went by, to the longer distances, 12- and 24-hours. In fact, I rode six at the longer distance, even managing to finish fifth in the Wessex event in 1965. I joined the then newly-formed 24-Hour Fellowship for a time and enjoyed immensely the series of get-together weekends held at various venues during the winter months. Against my better judgment I was talked into acting as its treasurer for a time, which I didn't enjoy at all as it was far too much like what I did for a living! Perhaps as a portent of what was to come I became involved in the production of our club magazine during the mid-Sixties and also wrote a few pieces for the *24-Hour Fellowship Journal* and others, all amateur productions of course but unwittingly setting the scene for my later ventures.

About this time we took up camping as a family, with a frame tent and a Dormobile, which gave us a great deal of freedom very cheaply. In those days the average site fee was under 50p a night for the whole caboodle, and as well as giving us some good holidays it enabled me to race in various parts of the country without leaving the family behind.

While all this was going on I was pursuing photography in not quite the desultory fashion that had characterised my final efforts at road racing, but nevertheless without any great sense of purpose, other than action photos mostly of my clubmates and pictures of the family growing up that every parent does with a camera. Particularly with the latter in view I had introduced myself to 35mm work with a Baldinette, a neat German folding model for which I paid five pounds secondhand. With this I made my first essays into colour transparency work. I had already done a little colour negative shooting when I did some pictures for my sister's wedding using the Selfix which, with its relatively large negative size, had produced quite pleasing results. Nevertheless, the Baldinette had its limitations, particularly with action work: as with the others there was no coupled rangefinder although I had used a separate rangefinder in the accessory shoe almost since acquiring the Selfix. However, leaning towards ever more serious action work, something more versatile was needed and a house move left me with a little spare cash which I spent on a Russian Fed, a copy of the German Leica rangefinder camera, but much less pricey. Nevertheless it was a good buy at the time, possessing an excellent lens and the all-important coupled rangefinder which projected coincident images into the viewfinder, making it simplicity itself to see when a moving image was in focus. Thus equipped I could start to try and emulate the photographs I had so admired for a number of years in Jock Wadley's *Sporting Cyclist*, many of which came from the lens of Bernard Thompson. As it happened I came to know both these men well in later years when we were all in the swim together, as it were.

Cynthia had suggested to me some years previously that I ought to follow the lead of the photographers mentioned earlier and take pictures at races to sell to individual riders, but I was not then confident in my abilities nor in the adequacy of my equipment and also shied away from the expense of setting up a darkroom; use of commercial processing would have put it quite out of court, in any case. But now, I am at the turning point with which I started this introduction. I began to consider the idea seriously after a conversation with a chap cleaning the office windows who told me he had just set himself up in just that manner and had paid

for it out of his first venture by selling pictures taken at a school function to doting parents. Thus was my mind made up. I bought an enlarger 'on the knocker', blacked out the bathroom and got cracking, buying bulk film, paper and chemicals very reasonably from a mail order firm called Polysales, who I believe are long gone. Nevertheless, they served my purpose and I was soon selling to numerous competitors in local events, more than enough to cover my costs within a very short while.

More importantly in the long term, I elected to lay out some of that profit belatedly on a course with Mallinson's, mentioned earlier, which turned out to be the best money I ever spent. There was much good advice contained in it over a couple of years – emphasis on the need to study prospective markets, the way to approach editors, the obvious need to produce the best work of which one is capable and, quite importantly for those like myself with families to support and only limited funds available for extra-mural activities, that it is not necessary to buy the most expensive equipment to produce saleable results. As long as it is of good quality it's 'the bloke wot presses the button' that truly counts. In other words I was pointed in the right direction.

*   *   *   *   *

As with many opportunities in life, luck has its part to play. Many of the riders who were my picture customers I had known for a number of years and one of these was Eddie Cook, a near neighbour at that time and a national BCF cycling coach to boot. Incidentally, he later became editor and publisher of *Jazz Journal*. At that particular time, 1970, he had been asked by the editor of *Cycling* to do a series of articles on weight training and needed someone to take some pictures to accompany them. He had been impressed with my action work and asked me to do the necessary, which involved a couple of photo sessions at his house, and subsequent publication in the magazine, much to my gratification, the more so as even before they appeared a couple of months later I received a phone call from Ken Evans, then editor of *Cycling*, asking me if I would like to take on photographic coverage of events in the Essex area. Well, can a duck swim?

I gave up any pretence at racing myself after many years of effort distinguished by a consistent mediocrity, and was launched on a new career alongside the day job, photographing local road races and time trials and within a couple of months had been elevated to covering the prestigious Smirnoff Scramble, a premier cyclo-cross event held at Harlow. This work sometimes involved a Sunday night trip to *Cycling*'s office which was then in Fleet Street, to hand in my film for processing in their labs and either wait for it to be returned after choice of usage had been made or pick it up the following day as I was working only a short distance away in the City. As a freelance I retained copyright and could then use my pictures as I wished. If there happened to be a staff man doing the event report I could hand over my film to him, so saving myself a trip to Fleet Street. Not that I minded those visits to the office; I got to know the people involved in the production of the magazine, editor Ken Evans, seemingly young but very much on top of the job, deputy editor Sid Saltmarsh, much older and formerly cycling correspondent of a long-vanished daily newspaper. He had the reputation of being an old grouch but I got on with him well. My family will say it's a case of like attracting like, but I think he appreciated that I was learning the ropes quickly and just wanted to do a competent job. Indeed I learned a great deal in a very short time from both Ken and Sid.

Others more junior on the staff at that time were Phil Liggett, later to go on to organise the Milk Race and to a career with television, Steve Coffey, Les Woodland, Keith Bingham, who has recently retired from the magazine, and secretary Marje, whose main job on a Sunday night was to take down race reports phoned in by correspondents all over the country. There was always plenty of banter going on and other freelances coming and going with their material. Among them was Alan Gayfer, a former editor of the magazine and an early contributor to *Sporting Cyclist* under the pseudonym C.C. Lawrence. He and I became good friends as I did

with Mal Rees who had recently given up his cycle shop in West London in favour of a freelance career: "Gave me twenty years of bloody hell!" was his verdict on the cycle trade in his strong Welsh accent, "and now I'm enjoying myself." As was I.

In fact, while often producing good work, Mal had a reputation for mishaps, such as forgetting to put a film in his camera, which he did once when I was working beside him, bringing forth some more choice Welsh expletive.

The Mallinson's course had emphasised the importance of keeping a weather eye open for every opportunity of selling a picture and after a few months of regular race photography I happened to be at a local club time trial where the timekeeper, Keith West, was using a computerised timing device made by himself. This was in the early days of computers and open events were still required to be timed by certificated chronographs. Nevertheless this seemed an interesting pointer to the future and, bearing in mind Mallinson's advice, I submitted a picture to *Cycling* with an extended descriptive caption. This was accepted and a short time later I received my usual instructions for the following Sunday's photography together with a commission to do the report also! And from there on my work became two-pronged, sometimes doing the pictures, sometimes doing the report, more often doing both, and occasionally, if it were a major event, a rider interview as well.

I soon discovered there were other outlets, too, with local newspapers, which would frequently accept a picture of any rider from their coverage area who had done anything of note, and these made a useful spin-off for work already done for *Cycling*. I also got cycling-based articles published in the rather unlikely pages of *YMCA World* and *Practical Photography*.

At about this time, with the family now well established, I felt could indulge in serious touring again after a lapse of some twenty years and initially at the instigation of my clubmate Paul O'Kelly, I embarked on the series of expeditions both in Britain and later on the Continent which provided me with the material for the many touring articles which

I wrote over the ensuing twenty years. At first I had approached this sort of material with caution, having read many other touring writers, some deadly serious, others such as Rex "Ragged Staff" Coley, whom I would later get to know, using what I can only describe as a jolly *Boys' Own Paper* style. I tried to hit the middle road with a fairly light-hearted style while still giving some impression of atmosphere and commentary on whichever area I was concerned with. This seemed to go down well from the start and I continued in much the same vein until certain changes came about. But more of that later.

As a result of my increasing involvement with events of all kinds I obviously got to know a great number of people and was soon privileged to be invited by team managers such as Bob Fowler and Tom Gargett to accompany them on racing trips to France and Belgium, sometimes with teams of young riders to widen their experience, sometimes with seasoned competitors as with a visit to Luxembourg on a try-out for a World's Championship road team. They obviously expected some publicity from my presence which I was only too happy to provide. There was always plenty of material to work on and sometimes I was able to produce two separate features, one for *Cycling* and another on a completely different aspect of the trip for *International Cycle Sport*, the successor to *Sporting Cyclist.*

Others I got to know quite well were Ron White, cycling correspondent of the *Daily Express* and the driving force behind the building of Harlow track. I also became on very good terms with David Saunders, correspondent for the *Daily Telegraph* and TV commentator. He seemed to take something of a shine to me and sometimes, if he was abroad covering an event on the Continent, he would ring up and ask me to stand in for him on some important home race if it was within my area. I was only too pleased to do this as I would probably have been there on behalf of *Cycling* or *ICS* anyway, and thus I appeared in the *Daily Telegraph* as 'A Special Correspondent'. Unfortunately this came to an end with David's tragic death in a car crash in 1977.

Another I came to know particularly well was Vin Denson after he returned from the Continent and settled with his family in Essex. In fact we were clubmates and spent much time together both on and off the bike and on family camping trips and the like for a number of years. He featured in several of my touring articles as the Old Pro. Curiously, he makes no mention of this whatsoever in his book *The Full Cycle* despite using several of my photographs which I had given to him as mementos over the years.

*   *   *   *   *

Although much of my work was with relatively minor events, I was involved with two of the most prestigious races during the Seventies. The first was the Tour de France in 1975, the first time it came into Paris to finish on the Champs Elysées. Peter Fretwell, publisher and editor of *ICS*, was unable to go and asked me to go in his place. The cycling press were entertained in the Club Pernod overlooking the Champs Elysées during the whole of the final stage which enabled me to write a story with something of a different slant although I was some what restricted as to photography with an estimated half a million people cramming the barriers below.

The other event was the Milk Race of 1978 when Phil Liggett, by then the organiser, invited me along as an extra official photographer for that 21st anniversary event. It was an interesting experience, spending a fortnight in an officially-allocated Range Rover complete with driver, much of the time with Bernard Thompson who was photographing for *Cycling*. My overall impression, though, was that the race was too long, the powerful East European teams had it sewn up within about three days and spent the rest of the race sharing out the prizes among themselves which made for a rather boring event. Certainly I have always felt that it was too long to keep the Great British Public interested. It would have been far better in my view to have concentrated on developing the end-to-end character of the BLRC's Brighton-to-Glasgow, six or seven days of which was just about enough to hold the GBP's attention.

By the early Eighties editorship of *Cycling* had passed to Martin Ayres, with whom I established a very pleasant working relationship. Present editor Robert Garbutt became assistant editor and my old friend Dennis Donovan had also joined the staff after a spell editing *Counties* magazine, the amateur journal of the Eastern Counties CA. At about the same time another journal appeared on the scene, a monthly entitled *Pro-News*, published and edited by John McKenzie, who owned a company called Midland Letterpress which sponsored the Coventry Olympic club. His editorial policy was bitingly critical of the cycling establishment, scurrilous even, and there seemed to be some antipathy between himself and Peter Fretwell of *ICS* who reportedly let it be known that if any of his contributors wrote for *Pro-News* they would never appear in *ICS* again. I thought this a little high-handed and as John had asked me to do race reports for him I went ahead and wrote them under a pseudonym. However, his magazine lasted less than two years. Financial difficulties were indicated by reluctance to cough up fees promptly after a year or so and the whole venture came to an abrupt halt when John, only in his mid-forties, died suddenly of a heart attack, doubtless the result of business worries. Oddly enough, *International Cycle Sport* lasted only another eighteen months or so, which was a pity as I felt that I had done some of my best work for Peter Fretwell.

Almost simultaneously with all this I had received a phone call quite out of the blue from Richard Ballantyne of *Richard's Bicycle Book* fame asking me if I would like to contribute a regular piece to a new monthly he was launching under the title of *Bicycle Magazine*. Naturally I accepted, particularly as he was offering generous fees, and for two years or so I wrote a series of articles on various aspects of the cycling game until Richard sold his interest in the magazine and a new young editorial team had different notions and my contributions came to an end.

However, *Cycling,* later to become *Cycling Weekly,* was still soldiering on and I had a very fruitful ten years or so under the Ayres editorship. Incidentally I always thought the change of name was a mistake as it immediately became lampooned as 'Cycling Weakly'! And then in the early Nineties, with Martin moving on, a certain Andrew Sutcliffe, formerly editor of *Cycle Trader* took on the editorial chair and things began to change radically. My own opinion has been confirmed by others recently that Sutcliffe had no real interest in the cycling world, and was only using it as a stepping stone to further his personal ambitions. Anyway, it was obvious from the start that long-established freelance contributors were gradually being elbowed out in favour of young come-latelys and even within the staff ranks there was discontent among the older members as reported quietly to me by Dennis Donovan. He also told me that there had been some sort of directive to the effect that "we don't want any more of this old stuff!" presumably a reference to the grass roots contributions of the likes of me, Albert Winstanley Nick Loasby and others. There was a reluctance to pay fees promptly – Bernard Thompson had trouble with this as well – and within a short while I was told very abruptly that my pictures were no longer required and that all local race reporting would henceforth be done through Graham Snowdon of Snowdon Sports Editorial. I went along with this for a while but it was soon obvious that all the work I was getting was writing shortish reports on local time trials on the same course week after week, and all without even a by-line, which I regarded as something of an insult considering the number of major features I had contributed over some twenty years. As a result I severed my connection with the magazine in 1993 and have never renewed it.

In fact, having taken a welcome early retirement from the banking industry some years earlier, I felt there were other things to do. I had the temerity to teach creative writing in adult education for two or three years but having given the Sutcliffe regime the heave-ho I got down to writing a couple of cycle touring guides to Essex, thinking that my connection with competitive cycling was at an end. However, another surprise was waiting in the wings. I was contacted by Colin Coe, another long-time acquaintance, who was very dissatisfied with the direction *Cycling*

Weekly was taking and, with assistance from Alan 'Knocker' Shields was setting up a new monthly publication to be called *CycleNews* and would I like to be involved with it? Naturally I was and within a short time got back in the swing of things. Run by people very much in touch with grass roots as well as the top echelons of the sport the magazine turned out to be a lively, broad-based publication with contributors well versed in the cycling world and I thoroughly enjoyed my connection with it. Unfortunately, advertising revenue was well short of requirements and regrettably the venture folded after a couple of years. None of us made any money out of it, indeed I suspect we were all actually out of pocket, but it was good while it lasted.

*   *   *   *   *

At this juncture I should go back to some comment on photographic matters during the years described. Some while before I embarked on my connection with *Cycling* I had scraped together enough funds to buy a second-hand top-of-range Yashica twin-lens reflex camera, following Mallinson's advice that a good big'un will beat a good little'un. The Yashica was a Japanese-made copy of the German Rolleiflex, much cheaper though but nevertheless very good value. However, it had its limitations for racing work inasmuch as it lacked a pentaprism, making accurate focussing rather tricky and unless I stood well back from the subject, thus making the image on the negative undesirably small, or took only side-on shots, there was 'big front wheel' distortion , not so noticeable in cyclo-cross work but very obvious in road or track pictures. Although I did use the Yashica extensively to illustrate my touring features the obvious way ahead for competition work was through the 35mm single-lens reflex with its ability to use telephoto lenses and again I scraped the barrel to buy a Russian Zenith, one of the cheapest and simplest SLRs on the market but solidly made and, with the then popular 42mm screw-thread lens mount, making possible the use of a wide range of reasonably priced but nonetheless good quality lenses. It had

no metering but that had never been much of a problem to me as I had for years used a Kodak exposure calculator, surprisingly accurate, before moving on to a small hand-held selenium meter supplied very reasonably by the afore-mentioned Polysales firm.

I beggared myself to buy 135mm and 200mm lenses and soon began to make real progress as evidenced by the photos included here. As earnings mounted I moved up to a Japanese SLR marketed by Dixons under their trademark Prinzflex; I believe it was actually made by Ricoh. This had through-the-lens metering and the Copal Square focal-plane shutter which had metal blades and travelled vertically across the film plane. I used this fairly happily for a couple of years although I found the shutter release a trifle heavy and the lever-wind mechanism jammed up on two occasions, necessitating repairs. Fortunately I always carried the Zenith with me in reserve on jobs, so I was able to finish my work in those irritating emergencies

Following this, a cycling acquaintance who worked for Dixons recommended me to get one of the new models they were just about to market under the Chinon brand name which was exclusive to them. I took his advice and found it an excellent tool. It had all the features of the Prinzflex but was better made and with the universal 42mm lens thread I could still employ my existing range of lenses. It proved such a rugged and reliable item that I subsequently bought another one and nearly all the racing work I did from then on was done with those two cameras. Typically at an important event I would be carrying one fitted with a 135mm lens and the other with a 35mm wide angle, a combination which would cover pretty well any requirement that might crop up. Then, following my stint on the Milk Race during which I had seen Bernard Thompson using a Tele-Rollei TLR to take 6x6cm colour transparencies (always useful for cover work) I bought an early model second-hand Mamiyaflex, Japanese made and the only twin-lens reflex with interchangeable lens facility, together with 135mm and 180mm Sekor lenses. It was also able to utilise a removable pentaprism which put action work on a par with a 35mm

SLR. The lens quality was superb and I did actually manage some very nice action cover work with it but, despite its versatility, I found it a heavy camera and rather cumbersome in the field and in fact I was able to produce equally saleable work on the 35mm Chinons.

At the same time, like any absorbed photographer, I could not resist buying other cameras which interested me and one of these was a 35mm Kodak Retina which I bought from a clubmate. The Retina range was made in Kodak's factory in Germany and my particular model dated from around 1950 and was of the folding variety with the excellent Compur shutter and Xenar lens, a bargain at the five pounds I paid for it. It was a handy little camera to tuck away in a saddlebag or in a pocket for the odd chance shot and a couple of the photos included in this volume were taken with it. There were also larger format cameras from 3½" x 2½" to 5" x 4" which I bought in pursuance of a nebulous ambition to produce landscape work for calendars and the like, but I never seemed to find the time to get serious about that branch of photography although I was able to combine it with my touring articles.

*   *   *   *   *

With the demise of *CycleNews* my involvement with commercial cycling journalism effectively came to an end although I was still enjoying active cycling with the Forty Plus CC. At the same time I was able to hark back to my schooldays, when I and other friends had been involved with Meccano and Hornby trains, and give more time and attention to the railway modelling I had fiddled about with on and off since my own children had been small. Even later, when well established as a cycling journalist I had essayed a few small projects and produced some articles for the model railway press, but with plenty of time and funds I could now indulge myself in both indoor and outdoor layouts. This led to fairly regular contributions to modelling magazines but equally importantly in the light of modern requirements, to digital photography. I had initially regarded it somewhat dubiously, having seen early results made on what

the trade calls 'consumer equipment' which were not a patch on what I had achieved myself on film. However, technology was marching on apace and it became obvious that if I wanted to compete in the fresh fields that were opening up I should have to move in that direction. So, after some considerable research and consultation I lashed out on a good quality Canon DSLR and also a computer to act as my 'darkroom'.

I have to say that I am now a complete convert to digital: I can see my results immediately, the photographic quality is the equal of anything I have produced even on the larger format of 120 roll film and gone are the long hours in the darkroom which I used to enjoy but latterly were becoming tedious. I love the versatility and handling of the Canon and my one regret is that digital as now available was not around when I was doing all that work for the cycling press.

However, there are no other regrets about those years of portraying the cycling world through words and pictures. I loved every minute of it, it made my life very much more satisfying as well as more comfortable and I met people and saw places I would not otherwise have done. What appears here is a but a tiny fraction of the thousands of pictures I took. My chief problem has been not so much what to include as what to leave out and it might be asked why there are not more shots of major events such as the Tour de France and Milk Race. The answer is that these have been more than adequately covered by others, and in any case I was always just as happy covering minor events as long as I was involved in the cycling world, using my camera and my brains. What appears here is what has pleased me in the taking, what in many cases has pleased editors to use, and what I hope will please those who pick up this book and turn its pages. It's about the photography as much as the cycling and represents just a little bit of an old all-rounder presented for readers' delectation.

We start this miscellaneous collection with the famous Bomb Hole in Epping Forest, the result of a German V2 rocket falling here some time in 1944/45. The resilience of nature soon softened the raw outlines of the crater into the semblance of a natural pond and by virtue of its proximity to the A11 it soon became a popular stopping-off place for many of the cyclists who used that road. Some just stopped off for a brief lounge by the water but for others it became their principal destination for swimming and sun-bathing or just loafing about and debating issues of the day with their cronies. It's probable that many a promising racing career foundered in the inviting pleasures of this unofficial rural lido which its habitués even provided with a rustic diving board, visible on the left of my photo.

The picture dates from March 1954 when some of us paid a visit to inspect the Bomb Hole after the ravages of a harsh winter. It shows my preoccupation with the landscape scenes I had always admired in other photographers' work and comes from the very first film I ran through a newly-acquired Ensign Selfix, in replacement of the Kodak bought the previous summer and already showing its limitations.

Lounging by the diving board is my old school friend Don Warren who had been instrumental in introducing me to the world of club cycling some years earlier. Also in the picture, wearing shorts, are the delightfully eccentric Hollis brothers, Frank and Dave, stalwarts of the free-thinking BLRC membership.

Here is the first *successful* action photo I ever took. Using the top shutter speed of 1/300 sec. on the Ensign Selfix and managing to judge the focussing distance fairly accurately I captured a breakaway group in an Essex road race climbing the hill at Stapleford Abbotts in April 1954. The leader is Dave Lee with Tony Allen bringing up the rear. The middle rider is unidentified. It is interesting to observe the type of racing jersey used in the mid-twentieth century, provided with both front and rear pockets, the former seemingly expressly designed to swing about when loaded with food and also to catch any headwind going!

The art of panning accurately to capture a rider at relatively close range takes a good deal of practice and it was some years before I was even half satisfied with my ability to produce a shot of an individual rider in action. This was in part due to the lack of a coupled rangefinder or reflex focussing on the Selfix but nevertheless I managed to get a few reasonable shots at the RTTC national 100-mile championship in 1961. Although not perfect I include this photo because it is the only one I have of Ray Booty, who was the first rider to bring the 100-mile competition record under four hours and also topped the British Best All Rounder competition three times during the Fifties. By the time of my photo, having achieved those distinctions, he seemed to be less interested in top class racing and, by all accounts, leaning more towards serious touring and small boat sailing.

By the mid-Sixties I had become very involved with 24-hour time-trialling, both as competitor and as helper. On these latter occasions I always carried a camera and this photo, shot at Pease Pottage just off the Brighton Road, shows a typical period scene at the start of a Catford CC promotion in the mid-Sixties. It is taken from a 35mm colour transparency original taken either on a Baldinette or a Fed, I cannot now remember which, and pictures my clubmate Peter Reeve about to be pushed off on his twice-round-the-clock effort with Bill Sargent on a tricycle waiting his turn behind. The timekeeper is Alan Gordon, who, many years later and by then in his eighties, was a stringer for a London news agency and often used to ring me up for news on local Essex events. I suspect the pusher-off to be Norman Winter who was my next-door neighbour on the Essex coast for a time in the Nineties. The gent on the left wearing shorts and with arms akimbo is Jack Spackman, founder of the 24 Hour Fellowship and a decidedly eccentric character whose declared ambition was to ride a 24 for every year of his age.

This shot of Roy Cromack, an outstanding rider of the period, shows him in the Mersey Roads 24 of 1969 in which he became the first man to top 500 miles in such an event, his winning distance being 507 miles. He is seen here early on the Sunday morning after about fifteen hours in the saddle with the effort beginning to show. The photo dates from before I had launched into freelance work for magazines and was even yet endeavouring to perfect the art of panning to capture riders in action although I was good enough by then to be selling photos of themselves to individual riders. The camera was a Russian Fed, a copy of the German Leica, using the standard 50mm lens. This camera had a coupled rangefinder which made it much easier to focus on a moving rider. A certain graininess in the background was the result of using Orwo film, an East German product which, while cheap, lacked the finer grain of such emulsions as Kodak and Ilford.

Beryl Burton, in my view, was the most under-rated woman athlete in the world and never received the national recognition which was her due. She was a world champion on both road and track and dominated British women's cycle competition for more than twenty years. My photo shows her in the same event as Roy Cromack, the Mersey 24 of 1969. The previous year she had ridden the Essex Roads 100 mile time trial on the Southend Road course and recorded a time of 3.55.05, a women's competition record and faster than all the men's entry which included most of the top riders in the country. Some of them were not pleased! However, in the event illustrated, her first attempt at 24 hour competition, although reputedly in the lead for a considerable distance, she found the effort of turning her customary high gears too much over that mileage and retired around two-thirds distance.

A curious feature noticeable in this shot is her lop-sided grip on the handlebars. For some reason or other she always rode with her right hand higher up the bend than the left.

This unkempt-looking group of Buccaneers CC members are gathered somewhere in Essex in the aftermath of a night ride in the late Sixties. Those expeditions were the brainchild of Paul O'Kelly, scratching his ear in the photograph, and always took place in the dark nights of autumn, never in summer as might have been considered more sensible. There were several of these at that period and inevitably ended up in the small hours with the participants holed up for an hour or so's kip in a haystack or barn or similar. I recall one occasion when a novice member was too shy too bundle up with the rest of us in a hayrick and was discovered in the early stages of hypothermia, necessitating marching him up and down a lane for half an hour to restore his circulation.

The low angle of the photo indicates it was probably taken with my Fed perched on a wall making the exposure by means of the delayed action mechanism. Remembrance is now dim but I must have taken several varying shots here as some years later I used one to illustrate a short article I wrote for *Cycling* magazine on the joys (and otherwise!) of night riding.

In this shot I am third from the left wearing my old RAF cap-comforter and other vintage garb while the short chap at the back wearing a bobble hat is Gordon Attwell. Some ten years later he was run down and killed on the A12 while riding out to perform his regular function as timekeeper at a Saturday afternoon time trial. His death was a great loss to all who knew him as he was one of the most amiable characters one could wish to meet.

"What was your most embarrassing moment?" is a question we often hear asked. This is it for the man with his arms in the air here, my old friend and clubmate Paul O'Kelly. This was the Stebbing Carnival road race in 1971 and Paul threw the customary salute in anticipation of victory before he had reached the finishing line. However he reckoned without the wily Morgan Jackson who came up fast under his left arm to snatch the win by a tyre's width at the actual line which is just ahead of the riders, level with the young lad in uniform holding the flag. The moral here is, the race is never won until the line is crossed!

In fairness to Paul, the lesson was learned and there were many other occasions when he was able to take the plaudits deservedly.

This tandem pair of Harry Sharman (steering) and my own clubmate Peter Reeve were photographed soon after the crack-of-dawn start of a London-Great Yarmouth road record attempt in the early 1970s. They are depicted on the Romford ring road which was less than a mile from where we lived at that time so I was able to amble along to await their passage before returning home for breakfast. I used my Yashica TLR for this shot as its between-lens shutter allowed me to use electronic flash at the fast shutter speed required to stop the action

The machine they are using is a Claud Butler Shortbase racing tandem, a product of one of the best-known specialist cycle builders in Britain from the 1930s to the end of the 1960s. His motto was "Champion's Choice" and indeed he supplied the machine on which the great Reg Harris won his first world championship. The Shortbase tandem was one of his most esteemed products; apart from its correct geometry and sturdy yet responsive construction, the essential feature was the short rear triangle, obtained by curving the rear seat tube, thus shortening the overall wheelbase, an important point with tandems, which tend to drag on hills. The one disadvantage is that it places the rear rider directly over the back wheel, thus subjecting him to more road shocks than with a longer machine.

Another important point is the large diameter, circular-section tube between the two bottom brackets. Latterly, most manufacturers have substituted a flattened-oval section tube here, for no good reason it seems as such tandems whip visibly under the efforts of two strong riders.

The frame of this machine is possibly pre-WW2 but, apart from the steel chainsets, it has been updated with much later equipment.

The 1970s brought a number of tours with groups from Essex which as well as being thoroughly enjoyable provided a rich source of photographic material for various publications. These became known as 'detraining tours' as most of them took place in autumn after the racing season was over and provided generous income for various brewing companies up and down the country!

One of the best of these was a trip to the Lake District in November 1972. Partly because of very wet weather and partly due to the terrain our mileage was by no means great, but pleasure should never be measured by distance alone. One rather strenuous expedition was the rough-stuff crossing of the Old Corpse Road from Boot in Eskdale to Wasdale Head over Burn Moor. The ascent from Boot was mainly rideable but the somewhat precipitous descent into Wasdale was very tricky in persistent rain and the first of my pictures shows my clubmate Alan Dawson negotiating a slippery beck on the way down.

By contrast, the second photo is of some of the party relaxing by the waterside after our arrival at Wastwater youth hostel later that afternoon. This scene, looking northwards towards Lingmell and Great Gable, harks back to my early interest in landscape photography, demonstrating that sometimes elusive recession of planes, as well as capturing a mood of tranquillity and satisfaction after a testing day among the hills.

Both shots were taken with my Yashica TLR on fine grain Ilford film and both featured in illustrating a subsequent article I wrote for *Cycling* under the title 'Cockneys in Cumbria'. The entire series I took on this particular tour gave me great satisfaction. I was able to use the shot of Alan Dawson in another piece I wrote some time later about rough-stuff cycling for a magazine called *The Great Outdoors*, and other pictures, held on file by *Cycling*, popped up from time to time to illustrate particular items.

One of the hardest tests of a time triallists ability is to ride alone on a place-to-place record with no other riders to provide the spur of competition. Nevertheless there are always cyclists ready to pit themselves against the clock alone. The early Seventies saw a series of attempts by Essex riders on the Road Records Association London-York figures, none of them successful, unfortunately. I followed several of these from a seat in the observers' car in my capacity as reporter and one attempt in particular sticks in the mind as a very gallant failure. This was the ride of Graham Mann of the Hainault RC who was on schedule for a narrow beating of the existing record for some 170 miles of the 200 mile distance. This saw him as far as Selby, where the River Ouse is crossed by a swing bridge and it was always understood by the authorities that they would obligingly hold any opening of the bridge until the rider had got through. This was done, leaving Graham the tightest of margins for the last miles into York. And this was where the loneliness of the long distance cyclist took its toll, those of us in the observer's car watching him struggle valiantly against the relentless clock only to reach the finish in York totally spent and just three minutes outside the existing record.

My picture shows him utterly exhausted and disappointed after being helped from his machine at the finish by national coach Eddie Cook, manager for the attempt. It is a graphic illustration of the demands made by what is demonstrably one of the hardest of all sports.

Eddie Cook, incidentally, as mentioned earlier, was the man responsible for getting me my opening with *Cycling* magazine and earned my gratitude for opening up a new phase of my life.

The programme involving the junior championship (page 30) also included a senior road race and it was while out in the countryside getting the required photos that I realised I was standing alongside the bridge which had been the scene of the Great Train Robbery ten years earlier. Thus I made a particular point of including it in this shot and wrote a couple of paragraphs round it, making a separate item in *Cycling* a couple of issues later. The leading rider in the bunch coming through the bridge is Alaric Gayfer, son of Alan Gayfer, a former editor of *Cycling*.

My picture here is of the finish of the 1973 national junior road race championship at Mentmore Park which I reported for *Cycling*. It was my experience throughout my long connection with cycle racing that junior events nearly always resulted in a bunched sprint finish. This is because, despite obvious ability in many riders, they lack the experience and confidence to go it alone and prefer the shelter of the bunch and the chancing of their arm in the hurly-burly of such a finish as illustrated here. Nevertheless this was an exciting sprint and one which presented me with a shot which comes high on my level of satisfaction. The elation on the face of winner Brian Ellis is very obvious as are the expressions of effort on the faces of those in the milling bunch.

It appears that I am standing in the road right in front of the riders but in fact I was positioned a good distance beyond the finishing line shooting with a 200mm lens on a 35mm SLR. Somewhere in this bunch, incidentally, is Steve Lawrence who went on to become one of the top senior road riders of the later Seventies and early Eighties.

Much of my regular work for *Cycling* at this period was concerned with coverage of time trials in my own local area around Essex. Sometimes these were accorded championship status as is the case with this picture, another of Beryl Burton, somewhat later than the earlier photo but still when she was at the height of her powers. Here she is on her way to yet another 25 mile title and I have caught her in full flight using the Yashica TLR with fill-in electronic flash. Action work of this type was not always successful with that camera as it had no provision for a pentaprism so I had to prefocus on a particular spot and, looking through the direct vision finder, trust to my judgment to hit the shutter release at precisely the right moment. In this instance it came off and Beryl's extreme concentration is clearly evident as is her lop-sided grip of the handlebars as noted previously. However, there were other occasions when I was not so lucky and soon after this I abandoned the use of the Yashica for racing pictures and employed a succession of 35mm SLRs.

A trip I did on three or four occasions with various groups during the Seventies was to do an illustrated feature on a big race in Northern France still known as Les Quatre Jours de Dunkerque, although by that time it had been extended to six days. It always drew a top class field and one of the best vantage points was the town of Cassel which crowns a prominent hill rising from the plain of Flanders. The race passed through the town several times, thus offering ample opportunity for varied photography. The first of my pictures was a grab shot taken while we were awaiting the arrival of the race and shows two young fans in suitable headgear, the little girl visibly impatient, frowning and shrugging because the riders were not yet in sight. I had a 200mm lens fitted to my SLR which enabled me to snap the children without them being aware, the narrow depth of field also separating them sharply from the background.

The second photo, also with the 200mm lens, shows the leading group on the climb into the town with the car of the directeur de course in close attendance followed by an armada of team support vehicles, my long lens compressing them into a forest of spare machines, quite appropriate given the tree-lined nature of the road..

The third picture is in the town itself, on a downhill corner which left no time for sizing up a shot so I prefocused and ripped off exposures as fast as I could, giving thanks for the lever-wind and feeling fairly sure I would get something useable. Indeed that proved to be the case as witness this shot which has the legendary Eddy Mercx dead centre. This set of exposures was actually on colour transparency film and another frame caught Freddie Maertens and Barry Hoban, a shot which was used in colour in *Fall from Grace*, the book about Maertens' controversial career. They also hark back to a time when riders were easily recognisable in photographs such as these in the days before they were all garbed alike in semblance of spacemen!

Expeditions such as those to the Quatre Jours often combined a bit of touring with various companions and I was always on the lookout for items of humour or other interest. I managed to combine both in this picture which was taken near Haverskerke in Flanders when we had stopped for lunch at a little country café. The proprietor had welcomed us cheerfully, regaling us with stories of the war and introducing us to two farm workers who were planting potatoes with a horse-drawn drill in an adjoining field. After every trip up and back they came into the café for a glass of wine and a chinwag and once well mellowed they were easily persuaded to pose for a series of photographs. The one reproduced here shows our host and the two workers posing with our bikes while ex-pro Vin Denson holds the horses' heads, Ed Pheby sits on the drill and sometime event promoter and team manager Tom Gargett beams at the right. One picture from this series appeared in *Cycling* as part of a feature I did on touring in Flanders and another made it into *Country Life* magazine.

The Welsh border country has long been a favourite touring area with me and has always provided plenty of photographic subjects. And in much the same vein as the potato planting I spotted the Back Ends road sign near Welshpool and persuaded some of our party to pose in this slightly 'robust' attitude. The humour was appreciated by *Cycling* where it was used as a 'filler' item some time later.

On a slightly more serious note I spotted an odd machine in the garden of a B&B at Peterchurch in the Golden Valley. This turned out to be a hand-operated sheep shearer, incomplete as it lacked the flexible shaft and clippers which were its business end, but it was of interest as it had been made by Lister in Dursley, possibly in the same factory which had played a part in producing the Dursley Pedersen bicycle. Certainly it used bicycle chain and Mick Henighan is here trying to count the teeth on the enormous chain wheel in a humorous attempt to calculate the gear. This photo appeared in *Country Life* and another from the series in *Cycling* with my appropriate comments.

The third photo from the Welsh border shows our party embarking on a rough-stuff crossing in the Berwyns which resulted in a headlong descent on a rock-strewn track in the pitch-dark into Llangollen. This again accompanied one of my touring pieces in *Cycling*.

The great point about these three shots is that it is not essential to have the most expensive equipment to take saleable pictures. All three were taken on inexpensive though well made 35mm cameras, the sheep shearer on a Russian Zenith SLR and the other two on a second-hand folding Kodak Retina.

Early in 1973 Bob Fowler invited me to accompany a team he was taking on a day's trip to Belgium to compete in a cyclo-cross promotion at Middelkerke, near Ostend. This was a flying visit in the truest sense as we crossed the North Sea by air using the now defunct Channel Air Bridge service from Southend to Ostend. It was a novel experience for all of us to watch the bicycles being loaded aboard the old Douglas DC4 car ferry as depicted here and then climb aboard almost casually, a far cry from the frustration which now seems a permanent feature of air travel.

On arrival at Middelkerke we were welcomed into the casino, whose owner was sponsoring the event, for morning coffee before the riders signed on in a local café. My picture shows John Atkins having his entry checked by a typical Belgian, complete with bargee cap and glass of beer conveniently to hand. Atkins was for many years one of the top performers in British cyclo-cross, winner of countless events and many titles, but on this course on which fast cart tracks alternated with loose, shifting sand dunes he was no match for world champion Eric de Vlaeminck, a rider who had a somewhat controversial career but when on form was unbeatable.

My pictures of these two were taken from the top of the dunes with a 200mm lens showing skilful Atkins making good use of the firm grass on a corner while de Vlaeminck, bicycle shouldered in expert fashion, makes light of the soft going with fellow Belgian Norbert Dedeckere concealed behind and bidding for second place.

Norbert "Nobby" Dedeckere was a popular visitor to Britain during the Seventies, along with several other Belgians, and scored more than one win in the prestigious Smirnoff Scramble held at Harlow every autumn. Like all top Belgian cyclo-cross experts he was meticulous in his approach to any race, examining the course beforehand, and I never once saw him fall off in any of the numerous events at which I saw him in action. He exuded confidence, never appearing rattled and in my shot of him at Forty Hall he appears almost detached , having established a winning lead.

Another of somewhat similar temperament was British international Keith Mernickle, seen here also at Forty Hall, who first made his name in cyclo-cross at the tender age of eighteen, going on to a long and distinguished career. Like Nobby he had a businesslike approach, doing his homework beforehand and, often as not, dictating the course of the race in an unruffled yet forceful manner. In addition I always found him easy to talk to after a race and he was always happy to give his analysis without any hint of egotism.

My picture is typical of many I took of him, calm, yet intent on the task in hand.

Doubtless the attraction of cyclo-cross to a number of spectators was the possibility of spectacular tumbles. Forty Hall at Enfield was a popular course for major promotions during the Seventies as it was of a sporting nature and also contained some hazards to make the contest all the more testing. Doing my own reconnoitre at one of these events after previous heavy rain I discovered a soft 'mudhole' in the woods, a likely spot for mishaps and eye-catching photographs. And so it proved. Although most of the top competitors had sussed it out and were keeping warily to the edge some of the less experienced were coming to grief in spectacular fashion. I spent a couple of laps grabbing shots of these unfortunates, panning through with each rider, using a 50mm lens to obtain depth of field to cover possible routes, and timing the exposure to catch the unlucky ones in full flight as here, which was the best of the bunch and appeared in *Cycling* alongside my report. Incidentally, no-one was hurt in these misadventures as the mud was far too soft to cause any damage.

Forty Hall was a good course for hazards as there was also a watersplash which always drew a crowd of spectators hoping for someone to get a dousing. My picture shows Chris Dodd, a top cyclo-cross man of the period leading through skilfully without dismounting while those being overtaken stick cautiously to the shallows afoot.

Another brilliant cyclo-cross expert of the Seventies, now virtually forgotten, was Jeff Morris, a joy to watch in action and very competent on the road, too, as pictured here during a race in northern France. His success at cyclo-cross was undoubtedly due to the fact that, based in France during the summer like most Continental stars in this field he put in a full road season, thus maintaining a level of fitness which produced an ability to perform at a high level in any branch of cycle racing. Unfortunately, he developed a painful physical condition which affected his wrists, as can be seen here where he is obviously trying to minimise road shocks by turning his hands outwards off the handlebars. His enforced retirement from competition as a result of this meant the loss to the sport of a vastly talented rider.

July 1973 brought a further invitation from Bob Fowler to tag along on a weekend trip to the Continent, this time to Belgium with a party of junior riders. Only national junior cyclo-cross champion Martin Springer had ever competed out of England before and the idea, of course, was to widen their experience in a racing environment very different from that in Britain. The first day's racing, at St Eloois-Winkel, introduced them to the murderous stone setts which graced many town streets in both Belgium and northern France, made all the more tricky by intermittent heavy rain, and our youngsters were quite literally very shaken by the experience, particularly as junior racing on the Continent was all hair and teeth from the start, unlike the usual sit-in-and-sprint amble at home. The first of my photos shows a string of local juniors making use of the paved cycle path in St Eloois-Winkel to avoid the shining wet setts visible to the right.

The following day at Aarsele the lads had settled down somewhat and both the up-and-coming Ian Banbury and Martin Springer put in some fine aggressive riding to finish sixth and ninth respectively. Banbury had actually led out the final sprint to vociferous encouragement from the crowd. "Engels, Engels!" they roared, but inexperience had prompted him to go too early and he cramped up before the line, though he had the consolation of having his face mopped by a young lady spectator!

The second shot here shows Banbury, (centre) followed by Springer, in a determined breakaway effort with two local riders. The measure of their effort can be judged from the fact they are all 'down on the hooks'.

In 1975 I was invited by team manager Tom Gargett to go along with a team he was taking to compete in Les Boucles des Flandres, based at Hazebrouck near the Belgian border. My first photograph shows how this nearly ended before it had begun when the roof rack carrying three bicycles parted company with the car at 90 mph somewhere in northern France. Tom is ruefully examining what appears to be a tangled mass of wreckage, yet it is a tribute to the quality of the modern bicycle that damage was largely superficial and was soon rectified after sorting out the mess by a visit to the cycle shop of Emile Becquet in St Omer. Curiously enough, this was the second occasion on which I had experienced such an incident, 90 mph seeming to be a critical speed at which wind resistance overcomes solidity of attachment.

Having overcome the roof rack mishap the team came to the starting line in Hazebrouck with quiet confidence. The strongest man in the team was undoubtedly Bob Downs who had shown great ability as a junior rider and, after a season in Belgium getting to grips with Continental racing, was now beginning to shake the bars of his cage. By the time the race was something over half run Downs had ensconced himself in a breakaway group which was finally whittled down to just four, Downs and three local riders, all from the same team, which didn't auger well for our rider. However, Downs had got the measure of both the circuit and the opposition by this time and suddenly launched a devastating attack on a short hill which took him away for a lone victory and wreaked such havoc on his erstwhile companions that team-mate Mick Wishart was able to come through for a well-deserved third place. It was a satisfying result to a weekend which had at first seemed fraught with disaster.

My pictures show, first of all, Downs sensibly cruising at the back of the leaders and taking up a drink from Paul O'Kelly before launching his hammer blow. We had run short of drinks by this time and had gate-crashed a wedding party in a roadside café to scrounge some water. Typically, we were given enthusiastic assistance, such is the passion for cycle racing in Flanders.

The other shot is obviously of Downs giving the victory salute in the streets of Hazebrouck, followed in by an independent car with spare wheels in case of need.

These photos were taken with a 135mm lens which I had settled on by this time for most of my racing work of this type. It has the advantage of greater handiness than the longer 200mm lens as well as having a slightly greater depth of field, useful when taking groups on the move. Both this trip and that to St Eloois-Winkel/Aarsele were the subjects of features I wrote for *International Cycle Sport*.

The subject here is Steve Lawrence, who burst upon the road racing scene in the mid-Seventies and, teamed with Bob Downs, was a major force in road sport for the best part of a decade. His ability to cross a gap was astonishing and a joy to witness. There are innumerable photos of him in my files, but this particular one shows him in an early season race around 1980 clad in his national champion's jersey and well wrapped up against the wintry conditions. This particular shot comes from a 6x6 colour transparency taken with the Mamiya twin lens reflex which I had recently acquired. Unlike my faithful Yashica this had the advantage of interchangeable lenses, allowing me to use longer objectives for better perspective in this type of work, as well as the provision of a pentaprism which provides a right-way-round image and takes the guesswork out of focussing for action pictures. The between-lens shutter fitted to the excellent Sekor lens allowed the use of electronic flash as a fill-in light while still permitting a fast shutter speed to stop the action.

Here is a scene unlikely to be witnessed under present-day conditions as a tight-knit bunch of riders from several Essex clubs set out on a mid-winter training run in the early Seventies. The motorists seen here would have been quite used to coping with bunches such as this going about their strenuous business, but with the tremendous increase in traffic, twenty-first century drivers would be unlikely to tolerate groups of this size impeding their impatient progress.

The central figure here, wearing the Anglia Sport track top, is well-known Essex event promoter Derek Worsley, now regrettably no longer with us. He was the instigator and organiser of such prominent races as the Grand Prix of Essex, Ronde Anglia, and the Criterium des Vainqueurs and through contacts in Holland was responsible for several visits by Dutch riders to compete in events in this country. He also had contacts with the little town of Lumbres in northern France, where he is here depicted, and for several years was engaged in taking a team representing Essex to compete in a three-day stage race based there, the Trois Jours de Lumbres. In truth, although the team did include some Essex riders, Derek had no scruples in importing riders from other parts of England to represent the home county. I accompanied them on several of these visits and although, to my recollection, they were never crowned with any great success (there was some very tough opposition) it was always an enjoyable trip in very pleasant countryside with a friendly welcome from the local people. All in all it was a good public relations exercise. And for myself, having taken a bike with me on at least a couple of trips, I was able to cobble together some touring articles on a much neglected area for the pages of *Cycling*.

Another easily-visited race in northern France was the Circuit of the Port of Dunkirk. For some years this had a strong British entry, largely through the agency of Roger St Pierre who is at the time of writing a contributor to *Cycling Plus* magazine. As the title suggests the course for this event lay entirely on closed roads within the dock area of Dunkirk. In 1975 I went with the job of doing a story on the race for *International Cycle Sport*, travelling by ferry from Dover which deposited us within walking distance of the course. As it happened there was an ample dose of rain sweeping in intermittently off the Channel making an already tricky circuit even more exciting as there were numerous railway crossings, the rails greasier than ever under the downpour.

My first picture shows the part of the main group negotiating just such a hazard with one rider already having come to grief in the centre of the shot. The rider in the left foreground is Keith Mernickle, having a rare outing in a road event, his cyclo-cross experience doubtless standing him in good stead in such conditions.

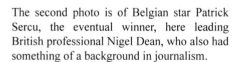

The second photo is of Belgian star Patrick Sercu, the eventual winner, here leading British professional Nigel Dean, who also had something of a background in journalism.

Also competing was former world pursuit champion Hugh Porter, here shown approaching a tricky corner with some caution. By this time in his career he had business interests – in fact he is riding a machine bearing his own brand name – and subsequently went on to a career as a race commentator. It is interesting to note in the light of present-day pampering of sports people that, like Reg Harris, Hugh was a self-made champion.

Note the straw bales beyond him, placed strategically to protect any rider misjudging the slippery corner.

Like most Belgians Patrick Sercu was very much an all-round rider and this picture shows him in action indoors in the Ghent Six-day event in the mid-Seventies. His sprinting power, both on road and track, was legendary and he was in the winning pairing of this event eleven times between 1965 and 1981.

As far as technical matters go, employment of electronic flash as the main light on an SLR camera with focal-plane shutter dictated the use a relatively slow shutter speed and although the speed of the flash has stopped Sercu, the rider in the background, lit mainly by the stadium lighting, has appeared as an almost transparent double image. The series I took at Ghent was something of a tryout as I was using 35mm colour transparency film to test the results of flash as the main light.

This photo appeared in *The Penguin Book of the Bicycle*, published in 1978, with the caption 'Cyclists with Saddlebags' in a section devoted to touring matters. However, all is not what it appears. The tall man sitting up in the middle of the group is actually the rear rider of a tandem which had broken down with a stripped freewheel and is being pushed and pulled by the rest of the party! Close examination will show the rider on the left using his pump to push against the saddlebag on the tandem. The location is somewhere on the North Yorkshire Moors during an autumn tour in the late Seventies and the exercise was no problem for experienced riders who found it all rather entertaining. I was in the saddle myself, taking the picture on the move using the Yashica TLR one-handed while steering with the other, using the zone focussing facility and viewing through the reflex finder; not as difficult as one might think.

I took this photo on the same tour, using the same technique, as our group was climbing Fleet Moss through a scattering of autumn leaves and both these pictures were used independently some time later in the pages of *Cycling* to illustrate various aspects of cycle touring.

Yet another picture from that North Yorks tour was this one of the ruins of Byland Abbey which we came upon in a misty dusk with the light failing fast and the prospect of successful photography receding. However, the camera was loaded with fast film and I felt it was worth a try at getting a result. Although my meter told me the fastest shutter speed I could use was 1/15th of a second, usually reckoned too slow for hand-held exposure, I held the Yashica firmly against a convenient fence post and took a gamble on it. And herewith the rather striking result which was used as a header to a two-part article I subsequently wrote for *Cycling* under the title 'Brown Splodge', a reference to the North Yorkshire Moors, or Cleveland Hills to give them their older name, as they appear on the old colour-shaded Bartholomew's half-inch maps. These attractive publications were ideally suited to cycle touring use but regrettably have not been available for many years.

The track at Harlow was the realisation of a dream for Ron White, cycling correspondent of the *Daily Express*. It was the result of around twenty five years of dedicated lobbying and fund raising and finally came to fruition in 1976 as an Olympic-size velodrome with 45 degree bankings and a surface of weather-resistant African hardwood, making it the only outdoor wooden track in Britain. Much of the work on the project was done by voluntary labour and I was very much involved with recording progress on film. The two pictures here date from early 1976 when laying of the surface had just been completed. The first shows Ron in happy mood pushing off Vi Denson on a child's tricycle, bought at a fund-raising auction the previous evening, thus giving her claim to being the first person to turn a wheel on the new track. The second shot shows Kath, Ron's wife, cheerfully engaged in sweeping dirt off the track ready for treatment with preservatives. The trackside barriers have still to be erected and the method of surface construction with longitudinal strips can be seen.

Once completed, Harlow track was in regular use for race meetings and my first picture here shows a Madison race in progress. This type of event involves teams of two riders, only one of whom is in competition on the track at any one time, and my picture shows partners handing over at the head of a fast-moving string. Shooting from the top of the steep banking like this with a medium telephoto lens gives a quite dramatic effect akin to aerial photography.

The steep bankings also made Harlow very suitable for motor-paced racing behind Dernys. The Derny is a sort of moped developed on the Continent specially for pacing work, on which the rider pedals continuously on a very high-geared single fixed wheel while the main power comes from a motor of about 200cc. They are also used on indoor tracks which are too small for big pacing machines, such as that erected at Wembley in past years for six-day racing. Dernys have also been used for pacing certain road races in France and elsewhere, notably Bordeaux-Paris and the Criterium des As.

The competitors in my photograph are using standard track racing machines, somewhat geared up, and it would be unusual latterly to see machines with reversed forks, as illustrated elsewhere, behind anything other than 'big motors'. Dernys are not fitted with distance rollers at the rear and it takes a highly skilled rider to lie close enough to the pacer to gain maximum shelter.

The machine illustrated here appears at first sight to have been involved in some kind of mishap but is in fact built specially for paced racing behind large motor cycles on hard, banked tracks. This spectacular form of racing, known on the Continent as *demifond*, was very popular in the early and middle years of the twentieth century, particularly in France and Germany, although in Britain there were few tracks capable of coping with the high speeds attainable behind the large motors.

This machine comes from the collection of John Malseed and dates from the 1930s when it was used by Charlie Bowtle, a well-known pace-follower of the period who moved on to pace-making after WW2 and was a familiar figure at Herne Hill in the late Forties and early Fifties pacing such riders as Wally Summers and Harry Grant.

The bicycle has reversed front forks and a 24" front wheel to enable the rider to get as close as possible to the pacing machine and thus obtain maximum wind shelter. In competition, a roller, set at hub height, kept the 'stayer' a regulation distance behind the rear wheel of the pacing machine and the best stayers held the front wheel as close as possible to this roller without actually touching it. For maximum shelter the rider sat well forward and the saddle is here mounted as far forward as possible with a support serving the dual purpose of steadying it and holding it at precisely the right angle for the rider's comfort. The large chainring provides the necessary high gear, about 120"as a rule and uses inch-pitch block chain, once very popular with track riders, being deemed more responsive than the standard half-inch-pitch roller chain. However, it has long gone out of favour and its distinctive tinkling noise is no longer an evocative feature of track competition.

I consider this photo of Dave Marsh at speed on the banking of Harlow track to be one of the best pictures I have ever taken. Curiously enough, although Dave was one of the outstanding riders of his day, it has never appeared anywhere other than here but in my view it embodies everything that cycle racing is about. Speed, effort, control, concentration, grit, all are captured here in a thousandth of a second through the 100mm lens of my Chinon SLR.

Leaving that aside it shows the classic form of the track racing machine as it existed from the 1930s until new concepts and new materials began to emerge a few years after this was shot in 1986. Brakeless, as required by regulations, it is short and fairly upright with large 5/8th inch diameter seat stays to give a stiff responsive rear triangle. Likewise the front fork tubing is of round section and short rake to eliminate flexing as far as possible under the stresses of high speed manoeuvring and to provide a vibrant, responsive machine.

The wheels are fitted with large-flange hubs which many riders believed to give a stiffer wheel to withstand the strains of sprinting and switching. Dave is also using double straps on his toeclips as an added precaution against pulling a foot out under extreme effort.

A greater contrast with Olympic-style tracks could hardly be imagined than the track at Paddington recreation ground. This dated back to somewhere around the turn of the nineteenth/twentieth centuries and was about a quarter of a mile round with the shallowest of bankings. Nevertheless it was always the scene of the keenest racing with a weekly evening league competition throughout the summer and a number of good quality promotions at weekends. It always drew a goodly crowd of spectators, partly because it was in an area of dense population and access was easy, and partly because entry to the trackside was free, being situated in a public park. Alas, like Harlow, Paddington track has disappeared under the onslaught of so-called council development.

Meetings at Paddington were always a rich source of photographic material and my picture shows the closest of finishes to a hotly-contested tandem sprint in the 1975 City of Westminster Grand Prix promotion.

For this picture the track scene shifts to Herne Hill and the traditional Good Friday meeting. The 1981 edition featured a revenge match between reigning world pursuit champion Tony Doyle and the man he beat for the title, Herman Ponsteen of Holland. Once again Doyle was victorious and the picture, one of a colour series I shot for *International Cycle Sport*, shows him doing his lap of honour on a road bike for some reason or other. It was always the custom since my earliest days of watching track racing to present the winner of a major event, particularly at a track meeting, with a bouquet of flowers. This probably derived from the Continent originally, and rivals in such races would always shake hands in gentlemanly fashion after crossing the line, left hand to right hand , while circling the track to wind down, a far cry from the hooligan exhibitionism of present-day competitors in many other sports.

This is a scene from a mid-Seventies race in Finsbury Park which has been used intermittently as a venue for closed circuit road racing from the days of the BLRC in the 1940s; in fact I rode one of my earliest races there in 1950. This shot is of a bunch negotiating the hairpin bend at the lowest part of the circuit before the long climb up to the finishing line. This particular spot has been the scene of more than a few pile-ups as it is preceded by a long downhill run necessitating some furious braking before a leap out of the saddle to tackle the climb. On a circuit of less than a mile and a half this can become very testing to say nothing of the pigeons which were prone to fly up into the middle of a hurtling group, as happened on my only venture there. The race depicted was one of a number promoted by a local paper, the *Islington Gazette*, and I landed the pleasant task of doing previews, reports and pictures for them.

In the summer of 1971 we took our children on one of our regular camping holidays, on this occasion to West Luccombe in Somerset, just to enjoy the coast and countryside without involvement in any cycling activity. However, in that sort of environment it was inevitable that some aspect of the game would not be far away. Within a short time of our arrival we found we had for neighbours a group from the North Hants Road Club who were using the site as a centre for some gentle touring around the Exmoor area. They were quite happy for me to photograph them and it is obvious from the picture reproduced here that some are 'real' cyclists, as evidenced by their footwear complete with shoe-plates (I refuse to use the Americanism 'cleats'!) while other younger members are still in the tyro stage and being introduced gently to the pleasures of club riding and touring.

   From my point of view it was a fortunate encounter as I subsequently contributed an article on cycle camping to a tabloid publication then called *Camping Caravan Monthly*, which was the forerunner of a number of features I did for it on the subject of family camping both in Britain and abroad.

By 1977 our children had grown up enough to be left to fend for themselves for a week under the eye of our eldest daughter, by then married, and Cynthia and I took the opportunity of having the first holiday we had enjoyed by ourselves for over twenty years. With our bicycles and camping gear we motored to Blackmore in the shadow of the Malvern Hills and set up camp to use as a base for gentle exploration of the delectable Worcestershire/ Herefordshire countryside. I found the notion of base camping rather appealing after numerous previous expeditions with tearaway male groups where we had to carry all our gear every day from night stop to night stop. This began to lose its attraction and a settled base such as this became our preferred arrangement as we found we were able to spend more touring time together.

The photo of us outside our tent is one of several I took in a mock-up session before we set out on a day's ride, using the delayed action setting on the Yashica which was perched prefocussed on the camping table. I wrote a feature for *Cycling* using similar shots to those featured here, the other showing Cynth enjoying the view from high in the Malverns. As a result of this latter, an aggrieved reader wrote a letter to the editor castigating us as cycling on the Malverns is prohibited, true enough. However, it was pointed out that in fact we had wheeled our machines right across the range without throwing leg over saddle, thus technically committing no offence.

Luck and anticipation combined play a large part in the capture of satisfying action pictures and this balletic 'pose' is the result of just such a happy chance. Jeff Lewis is here handing up a drink on the move to Graham Adams in the Mersey 24-hour event of 1976 in which I was myself assisting other riders in the same way, as well as putting together a race report and taking relevant photos. I had prefocussed in anticipation of something of this nature but it was sheer good fortune that Jeff's elegant action coincided with the moment of shutter release. My customary 135mm lens gave the entire action good perspective and also pulled the subjects out from an out-of-focus back ground.

Much to my satisfaction this picture did indeed appear in *Cycling* some time later over a caption with a ballet connotation. Incidentally, Graham Adams was the instigator of the notoriously fierce Tandem Weekends.

In the sweltering summer of 1976 we took a camping holiday in the ancient town of Montreuil in the Artois region of northern France, partly to enjoy the coastal region around Le Touquet and partly to enable us to see a time trial stage of the Tour de France which would give me the opportunity to photograph every rider in the race. We positioned ourselves in the welcome shelter of some woodland which even so was hot enough for some local residents to spray the riders with a garden hose. In accordance with the usual TdF custom competitors were despatched in reverse general classification order. As it happened it meant that the most satisfying picture of the set came right at the end when Freddie Maertens, race leader at that time, came storming up the slight hill where we were stationed, nonchalantly tightening a toe-strap at the moment I pressed the shutter release, giving me the shot reproduced here. He went on to win the stage of something over 30 Miles at an average speed of just about 30mph, a remarkable ride on what was a very 'sporting' course. He lost the overall lead later to eventual winner, fellow Belgian Lucien van Impe, but nevertheless gave me a very useful picture to use with an article I wrote for *International Cycle Sport* comparing the Continental approach to time trialling with the way we did it here.

It appeared in monochrome in ICS but the original was shot on colour transparency film with a 135mm lens and it was later used in colour in the book *Fall From Grace*.

Freddie Maertens featured in another favourite shot of mine, taken some three years earlier in the Quatre Jours de Dunkerque which he won on that occasion. Again he is featured in the time trial stage, again in the race leader's jersey, changing gear after negotiating a sharp corner over a canal bridge somewhere in Flanders. A photographic point of interest is that close examination of the photo gives the impression that he is using a front wheel smaller than the rear. However, application of a ruler will show that this is not so, it's a case of the camera fooling the eye, use of a 200mm lens in this instance exaggerating the perspective in a relatively close-up shot such as this. Although I was quite happy with this photo, which appeared in *Cycling* alongside my story on the race, I switched to the shorter 135mm telephoto thereafter for this type of work, partly to avoid the phenomenon noted here.

At Easter 1978 Cynthia and I were invited to Guernsey for the regular Guernsey Cycling Festival, all expenses paid by the Guernsey Tourist Board. Naturally I was expected to sing for my supper, but that was no hardship as we had a thoroughly enjoyable sojourn on the island, despite some ferocious weather, with the friendliest of welcomes and some hard-contested racing. The first shot headed my coverage for *Cycling* and shows a road race in progress along the exposed west coast of the island with an Atlantic gale roaring in and throwing everything it had at the riders, seaweed included, which can be seen flying up over the sea wall. Obviously this is a favourite picture of mine, combining as it does, landscape, action and atmosphere all in the one frame.

The second picture is of a rider tightening his toe-straps on the line at the start of a hill climb time trial on one of the steep roads within St Peter Port itself. Hill climbs do not permit a push start and there is a large stone placed behind his back wheel to stop him rolling backwards when released on the timekeepers "Go!"

The Festival always attracted a strong entry from the mainland as well as from neighbouring Jersey and my third picture reveals the social atmosphere at an evening function and shows my wife presenting an award to Glenn Longland, a regular and successful visitor here, with Eamonn Kennedy, one of the enthusiastic organisers, on the microphone. Chatting in the background are two other popular regulars, Peter Pickers and Willy Kirkland.

This shot was taken at the finish of the 1978 Goodmayes Wheelers 100-mile time trial in Essex and shows winner John Woodburn being congratulated by the late Sir Hubert Opperman, "Oppy" to everyone in the cycling world. Woodburn was an outstanding rider at all distances, and had RRA records to his credit at the time this was taken. He finished this particular season as British Best All Rounder and three years later became the only man ever to win both 12- and 24-hour titles in the same season. On first acquaintance he appeared taciturn but he was not averse to a pint or two in a local pub after an event and I always found him willing to open up with quiet good humour.

"Oppy" was an Australian who had enjoyed a successful career as a professional rider in Britain and Europe during the 1930s and had claimed several RRA records riding for BSA, but perhaps his greatest achievement was in winning Paris-Brest-Paris, a single stage race of over 700miles, without any team support, against the cream of Continental riders.

After retiring from racing he went into politics and became the Australian government's representative in Malta, subsequently receiving a knighthood for his services. He always retained his interest in cycling and was at this particular event at the invitation of a Goodmayes member who had spent time working in Australia and through being involved in cycling there had become friendly with Oppy.

This competent-looking rider is George Mount, one of the fore-runners of a number of American riders who were to make an impact on European racing in the later years of the twentieth century. He is pictured here in the Welsh mountains during the 1978 Milk Race, in which he finished fourth overall, riding a road-racing machine typical of the period c1955-1985. It is a bicycle of simple elegance: there is nothing superfluous on it, every piece of equipment has its appointed purpose and emanates a fitness for the task in hand. It is short in the rear triangle to provide the 'life' for hill climbing and sprinting, while the head angle is fairly moderate and the oval section forks are smoothly raked to give resilience with positive steering on winding, undulating roads. A spare tubular tyre is rolled up neatly under the saddle; it had been many years since riders coiled them around their shoulders and it is noticeable that George is not carrying a pump. Apart from the fact that this particular race would have had numerous support vehicles in attendance he probably has a compressed CO_2 pump stuffed into one of his back pockets.

The Milk Race always had a special vehicle and driver provided for official photographers and I shot this from the passenger window as we overtook. On account of the closeness of the subject I used a fairly wide-angle lens; I nearly always carried two SLRs, one with a telephoto and the other with a 35mm or 50mm lens attached and I was gratified to have this photo subsequently reproduced in an American cycling journal.

This pictures shows Alf Engers in a role which some might regard as out of character as he was largely regarded as a short distance 'dragstrip' performer who broke competition record several times at 25 miles in the 1960s, was a pioneer in the use of ultra-high gearing for time trials and also ran foul of authority for allegedly riding in the middle of the road to gain maximum drag from passing motor vehicles. However, there was more to Engers than that and later in his career he showed himself very competent in bunched racing and also in hilly events such as the North Road Hardriders' 25 over the Hertfordshire 'alps' which he won in 1977. He is here shown in the wet and windy 1978 edition in which he had to settle for second place after a tremendous battle with 1976 winner Bob Downs, then at the peak of his form and who still clocked the fastest time despite a puncture near the end.

Alf had the reputation of being unwilling to talk to journalists but I always managed a few quiet words with him, picking my time after the finish as I realised he liked to be left alone before a race to gather his concentration.

From a photographic point of view I always enjoyed hilly time trials as they offered so much opportunity for atmosphere and the depiction of extreme effort.

Such events as the North Road Hardriders' were the basis for the Sporting Courses Competition, 'Spoco', invented by my good friend Bill Norris in 1981. He had become disillusioned with the Best All Rounder type of competition, believing that it encouraged an obsession with times rather than the beating of other riders on any particular day. He arrived at the solution of a competition based on points gained in placings in selected time trials run over 'sporting' courses which were not based around dragstrips. I supported him in this and gave the venture as much publicity as I could in the cycling press, pointing out the growing artificiality of times recorded on ever more crowded main roads to say nothing of the dangers of ever faster moving traffic. I even edited and published a quarterly journal devoted to Spoco matters for a couple of years. However, the idea seemed to have limited appeal to dyed-in-the-wool time triallists and a large part of the entry came from road racing *aficionados* and 'mixers' such as John Patston who won the competition for the first three years of its promotion.

My picture shows him at the end-of-season presentation and disco in 1984 after celebrating with his team winners from Redbridge CC, Robin Gilham (L) and Rob Stahl.

London's Eastway circuit, now alas vanished under the new constructions for the 2012 Olympic Games, was well used during its existence and in the late Seventies hosted at least three promotions which brought top professional riders from the Continent to stimulate general interest in cycle racing among the Great British Public. Unfortunately, and perhaps predictably, the GBP did not rise to the bait and attendance at these meetings was mainly of the converted and not much higher than for a top class assembly of home riders. However, it gave those of us who were interested a chance to see the current Continental stars in action and I was there to photograph proceedings for the cycling press.

The pictures reproduced here are all from colour transparency originals: the first shows Gerry Knetemann of Holland and Francesco Moser of Italy leading a small group of home professionals. Knetemann is wearing his current world champion's jersey and went on to win the event. Was it fixed, one wonders?

The second shows Frenchman Raymond Poulidor leading Phil Bayton around one of Eastway's many bends. 'Pou-pou' came of peasant stock and probably for that reason was enormously popular with the French public, although he never quite achieved the success of some of his contemporaries, thus earning the nickname of 'The Eternal Second'.

My third shot is of Moser again, this time leading Dutchman Jan Raas around the sharpest bend on the Eastway circuit. This was christened Clarey's Corner soon after the circuit opened as well-known London rider John Clarey was the first to fall off on its deceptive curvature.

It is evident from all these photos that spectator attendance was not by any means what might have been desired.

These two photos come from a tour I made with old friends in 1979 in northern France, partly to see some of the Quatre Jours de Dunkerque and partly to have a good trundle round pleasant countryside in congenial company. The first shot is of Jim Larney and Don Warren on a quiet road somewhere in Flanders with a horse-drawn disc harrow in the adjoining field typifying the traditional methods of agriculture still holding good in France when such practices had long disappeared from Britain. From a technical aspect I was pleased with this picture as use of a 35mm wide angle lens had enabled me to use its great depth of field allied to a fast shutter speed to stop the action and at the same time keep the whole scene in focus.

The second picture shows us having a slightly bibulous lunch stop at a roadside café. John Fowle is chatting up Madame while Don Warren sits musing over his beer at the far end of the counter. The gent somewhat out of focus at the right is the late Peter Duker, journalist, author, jazz musician and generally rumbustious character. He was a scion of a northern brewing family but on account of his propensity for getting into bother it was said he was paid to keep out of the way, hence his frequent presence on the Continent. He claimed to have circumnavigated the globe by bicycle though this was disputed by some. However, I make no judgement as I always found him genial. We always seemed to meet somewhere around the Quatre Jours, usually in such venues as depicted here, and although he humorously confessed to pinching my material sometimes, the plagiarism was quickly put right with draughts of *vin ordinaire*.

Around the turn of the Seventies /Eighties I made several trips to Somerset with my clubmate Tom Booker who, in leisurely fashion, was looking for a spot to retire to. We had some thoroughly enjoyable tours, exploring the Quantocks, Mendips and Exmoor and I was able to indulge my ever-lurking penchant for landscape photography to the full, using the Yashica 6x6 TLR. One of the best to come out of this was the first photo shown here depicting Tom climbing up out of the Yeo valley on to the heights of the Mendip Hills after a tremendous rainstorm had just cleared. I made Tom wait while I got part way up so I could picture his ascent against the dramatic thunderclouds. It made a heading illustration to a feature I wrote for *Cycling* as one of several dealing with touring in the West Country.

The second picture came from a trip to Exmoor with Tom's teenage son Alan. My piece on this was entitled 'Escape to Exmoor'; here we were just embarking on some gentle rough-stuff and because of its completely accidental air of slight furtiveness this shot underlined the title and made the front cover of the issue of *Cycling* in which the feature appeared.

This photo of a group of Essex clubmen comes from yet another of my touring features in *Cycling*. Taken somewhere in the Cotswolds in March 1979 it illustrates typical Seventies cycling garb and a collection of touring machines typical of the period, all displaying a certain road racing pedigree but all fitted with sensible wide ratio touring gearing, driving 27" wheels shod with medium weight high pressure tyres. The machine on the left has an all alloy chainset, a combination of Stronglight 5-pin cotterless cranks carrying TA touring pattern double chainrings. Its owner has fitted his toe-clips with muffs to keep his feet warm and dry in wintry conditions.

The machine in the centre is built around an H.R. Morris frame and the ornate lugwork is just discernible. Dick Morris took over the Walthamstow premises of another well-known builder, F. J. Sanders, in the 1960s and quickly established a reputation for fine workmanship. Unfortunately he also established records in slow delivery and it was not unknown for a customer to wait five years for a frame to be completed! It says much for Dick's reputation that customers were prepared to wait that long.

As to the identities of the party, the bearded CB owner bending over the map is Eric Angell and the tall Morris owner in the centre is Graham Adams, both of whom were racing men to be reckoned with in the 1960s. The partly obscured individual at the back wearing a Campagnolo cap is former professional Vin Denson, by this time a keen amateur club rider once more.

At Easter 1980 myself, Cynthia and three of our daughters joined Vin and Vi Denson for a visit to Troyes in the Champagne region of France where Vin had started his career on the Continent as an amateur with a local club. We were made very welcome by his old manager, Didi Jacquelin and his family and also by other old acquaintances of the Densons. However the highlight of the trip was witnessing a fine win by a young English rider in the Grand Prix de St Parre-aux-Tertres. This was Malcolm Elliott, then virtually unknown and just beginning to feel his feet in Continental racing with one of the local clubs. It was his first win and was the jumping-off point for a long and distinguished career which included taking the Commonwealth Games road race title in 1982 and many other titles and victories during his racing years. I was in at the beginning, though. The first picture show him launching the attack which broke up the leading group with a lap to go.

The second picture shows him crossing the finishing line with the opposition spread-eagled behind him. Notice the crowd discipline and that photographers such as myself and the chap on the left are able to do our job without harassment from officious marshals or police as I experienced more than once in England. It was a great pleasure to write this up as a feature for *International Cycle Sport* and also use one of the pictures in *Cycling*'s 'Top Shots' feature for that year.

To the east of Troyes lies La Forêt de l'Orient which provided us with a tranquil contrast to the excitement of the racing scene which had formed a large part of our 1980 visit. The entire forest is a haven of peace and quiet, power boats are banned from the lake which it surrounds and at its centre is an area designated a 'Zone de Silence' where anything that makes a noise, such as motors, radios or musical instruments, is also banned. With its network of quiet, well-surfaced roads it is an idyllic touring area and, as a family, we made the most of it with some gentle riding during our brief stay. My third picture shows the Coulson ladies leaving the 'Maison Forestière' in the heart of the forest. This contains many exhibits relating to the history and development of the forest, and other exhibitions from time to time such as the display of macramé on show at the time of our visit, very interesting for the distaff side of course.

All this finished up as a touring and semi-nostalgic feature in *Cycling*, underlining what I had learned from Mallinson's many years previously, that a trip such as this can provide more than one string to one's bow.

At the beginning of December 1980 I received a phone call from Martin Ayres, then editor of *Cycling*, in a bit of a panic and asking me if I had any colour photos suitable for a Christmas cover as he had nothing on file. As it happened, neither had I, but fortune smiled for once and the following weekend we had a significant snowfall which obviously posed possibilities. Thus I set out to meet my clubmates for a lunchtime gathering at Pleshey, in the heart of Essex, trusting that some situation would crop up which I could turn to photographic advantage. And so it proved as, although only a few hardened souls had braved the weather, we discovered a snowman in the village street and I was able to get Eric Angell and Alan Flutter to pose for me for series of photos, one of which made the cover of *Cycling* for that Christmas and another, the one shown here, appeared on the cover of the Christmas issue of *Cycling World* some five years later.

I shot these on 6x6 colour transparency film using the Yashica TLR with fill-in flash to lighten the backlit shadow effect of the winter sunshine.

The Eastern Counties Cycling Association was formed in 1910 and has been a mainstay of cycle sport, mainly in the time trialling sphere, ever since. One of its most popular and enduring promotions has been the three-day Festival held over the first weekend in May. This was the brainchild of Redbridge CC's Alan Osborne and he has been its organising genius for over thirty years, finally relinquishing its responsibilities in 2010 at the age of 78.

The weekend always included a mixture of time trialling and road racing but one of the most popular and keenly contested events has been the map reading competition. My photograph, snatched with a 35mm lens on one of my Chinon SLRs, shows three young competitors getting down to it, quite literally, outside the event headquarters preparatory to finding their way around a maze of Essex lanes.

Quite early in its existence I wrote a eulogy high-lighting its appeal and friendly competitiveness for a short-lived publication called *Cyclist Monthly*, from the same stable as *Cycling*, edited by my good friend Dennis Donovan, like me a product of the Essex cycling scene.

The tricycle has always been a peculiarly British foible. No other nation uses the trike other than as a beast of burden and certainly not as an instrument of pleasure and competition. And to be sure, the tricycle is heavier than the bicycle, it presents a greater frontal area to a headwind and, despite possibly having ridden one in childhood those bicyclists later falling prey once more to the three-wheeler's indefinable attraction often find it a tricky beast to master in the early days of their infatuation.

Yet in Britain the tricycle has always attracted a dedicated following of enthusiasts and my first photograph shows a fraction of a social gathering of the Tricycle Association in the winter of 1980, with members obviously absorbed in appreciation of the finer points of other members' machines. Of the machines shown here, some are vintage trikes dating from the Twenties or Thirties, having the typical sloping frame angles of the period and retaining their Abingdon differential rear axles thus restricting them to a single fixed gear. Others are products of modern specialist builders, constructed in up-to-date geometry with lightweight steel tubing and derailleur gearing. Most of these modern trikes have no differential, the drive being taken to the left-hand rear wheel alone, which accounts in part for the tricky handling alluded to earlier.

However, one or two trikes have been produced with a double freewheel arrangement which ensures that whichever way the machine is being turned, the inner wheel is taking the drive, while on a straight course both wheels are driven.

The second picture shows some expert cornering by Les Lowe in the 1983 24-hour championship, throwing his weight over the inside wheel to hold it down as he negotiates a tight bend at speed. Les was the first secretary of the 24-Hour Fellowship and a dedicated mile-eater, it not being unknown for him to arrive back at his Midlands home at one o'clock on Monday morning after a hard-riding winter weekend in Wales. He recorded every mile he rode, as witness the cyclometer discernible on his front wheel.

Here is one of the leading lady distance riders of the early Eighties, Ann Mann, wife of Graham Mann, pictured elsewhere, on her way to a women's 24-hour competition record of 438.16 miles, a figure which stood for ten years. As with the photo of Les Lowe this was in the Eastern Counties CA national championship promotion in 1983, the first time the association had promoted at the distance for many years, and a very successful one at that.

My picture shows Ann early on the Sunday morning, still wearing arm-warmers against the night-time chill, out of the saddle as she climbs away from the flat alluvial plain of Thames-side Essex to cross the Southend Arterial Road *en route* for the hillier roads in the centre of the county. The effort of this twice-round-the-clock contest shows plainly on her face.

Some time in 1981 I saw in the RTTC handbook an advertisement for Whitfield frames, built by a certain John Weatheritt in the remote Hertfordshire village of Furneux Pelham. Intrigued, I telephoned John to enquire if he would be willing to let me do a feature on his esoteric business as part of a series I was doing for *Bicycle Magazine*. He was a little cagey at first until I convinced him there were no strings attached and I arrived one morning to a cautious welcome. However he warmed quickly on realising I had a genuine interest in what he was doing and that we also had other common interests such as preserved steam railways.

He had come into frame building after a career in engineering with the Ford Motor Company and Jack Brabham's development team. With a keen interest in cycling, as well as motor-cycles and cars, he found himself dissatisfied with frames ordered via cycle dealers and eventually decided to build his own. This developed into the business as I found it, with John working alone to produce high-quality silver-brazed frames in a large shed behind his cottage.

My photo shows him filing the lugs of a customer's frame to a feather edge before enamelling, a touch of refinement which marks out a craftsman-built frame. This one will have been built to special order as were all Whitfield frames. John was careful enough of his reputation to advise customers in detail on their requirements, whereas some other builders would make anything asked for, possibly resulting in a "dog's dinner" of a machine which was no credit to the builder or its owner. French bespoke builders, in contradistinction, had the reputation of refusing point-blank to construct anything of which they did not approve!

Incidentally, I asked John why he called his frames Whitfield instead of using his own name. Apparently that was his mother's maiden name and he wanted to avoid jokes about "Whether it's any good or not!"

In the first half of the twentieth century grass-track racing had been a popular branch of cycle sport for various reasons. From a rider's point of view it offered substantial prizes for a relatively brief effort; from a promoter's angle it required only a flat field with space for a circuit of around four laps to the mile and races could be, and often were, run in conjunction with athletic events. However, by the early Eighties the number of grass meetings had dwindled to a select few, one of which, though, still flourished, the meeting held at Mildenhall at the end of August every year. Grass racing was one of the few branches of the sport I had had little to do with and I paid my first visit there in 1983, surmising that there might be material there for a picture or two in one or other of the cycling journals. As it turned out I came away with a stack of good photos and was thoroughly impressed with a facet of cycle racing which was hard, go-all-the-way stuff. It obviously permitted no room for slackers and I wrote an illustrated feature which appeared in *Cyclist Monthly* lauding grass track as an ideal breeding ground for riders who had serious ambitions to reaching the highest levels of competition. A shining example is Victoria Pendleton who cut her competitive teeth here at Mildenhall and another was the now virtually forgotten Peter Brotherton, a world-class pursuiter in the Fifties, who was a product of the Lincolnshire grass tracks.

The first of my photos shows riders starting in a handicap event at Mildenhall, the gritted teeth showing the effort involved in getting the bike under way. The knobbly tyres, ideal for grass competition, can also be discerned on the leading rider's machine.

The second shot shows riders leaving the last bend *en route* for the finish, the leading competitor having a look under his arm to get the measure of his opponents.

I took both of these with my usual 135mm lens, crouching down to get the low angle which gives a picture a certain urgent impact.

A couple of years after my first visit to John Weatheritt, described previously, he phoned me to say that he was building a replica of a Dursley-Pedersen, a revolutionary design based on cantilever principles, which first appeared in 1893. Naturally I was interested and paid two visits, the first to see construction in progress and then to see the completed machine. I was privileged to be allowed an extended ride on it and also, for comparison, on an original brought along by Allan Hawkes of the Veteran-Cycle Club. This latter was obviously showing its age but John's machine, built in Reynold's 531 tubing and fitted with sprints and tubular tyres was a revelation in ease and comfort. These visits resulted in a feature in *Cycling* and my photograph is taken from a 120 roll film original which appeared on the back cover. It shows John pointing out some detail on his machine to a local clubman who happened along as we were doing a photoshoot in the village street.

For the record, John has moved to Scotland and no longer builds frames, but I am glad to say we are still in touch from time to time.

This illustration taken at a time trial finish at Hatfield Peverel in Essex shows the virtual prototype of what came to be known as the low-profile bicycle. It was developed by Norfolkman Mike Burrows, who later went on to collaborate with Lotus in producing the revolutionary machine used by Chris Boardman in his world championship and record rides. Here the 'test bed' machine is being ridden by Andy Pegg late in 1981, having one of its very earliest competition outings. In many senses this machine harks back to the 1920s philosophy of "as little bicycle as possible" and would probably not have looked out of place sixty years earlier. It was built specially to fit Andy, the large flattened-section seat tube running right up to support the saddle while the top tube meets it half way up, giving the impression of a child-size frame with a six-footer on board, an illusion heightened by the use of a 24" front wheel. Attempts at minimising wind resistance are evident in the use of the flattened handlebar section and the mounting of the single brake behind the fork crown. Clipless pedals had not long come on the scene and are employed here while, unusually for a latter-day time trial bicycle, transmission is by single fixed wheel, evidently in line with the rider's preference.

On this early outing the machine was received by other riders with a mixture of interest and scepticism, but other manufacturers began to follow the trend, sensing profit from fashion, and within a few years a large number of time trial bicycles were of a shape based on the machine shown here. I was assured, on speaking to the rider soon after photographing him, that despite the straight front forks and apparent 'monkey-up-a-stick' position that he had ridden the machine in a 12-hour event without any discomfort.

A later development of the low-profile time trial machine is ridden here by Tony Deacon and photographed by me on one of the popular Essex courses in 1986. As with the Burrows machine an attempt at aerodynamic streamlining has been made with the use of oval section frame tubing and curious handlebars of aerofoil section, the disadvantage of which is that they offer only one riding position. Any advantage gained by this design is probably psychological rather than physical as the main stumbling block with wind resistance is the human form itself.

The brake cables have disappeared as far as practicable within the handlebars and frame tubes and the rider is using clipless pedals , by then well on the way to ousting the tried and trusted toe clip. A fortuitous feature of this photo is that it has caught the stiffness of the frame causing the front wheel to leave the ground briefly as it passes over a protruding road joint.

This oddity is a tandem sextuplet constructed for the Rotary Club of Romford for use in charity fund-raising events and so on. Of necessity it needs to be strong and therefore contains a proportion of motor cycle components. It is noteworthy that the chain drive is on the left and it is also evident that the riders are not 'proper' cyclists as no-one has bothered to synchronise the pedals! The occasion was the opening of the controversial final phase of Romford's ring road in 1988.

This photograph was taken near Haarlem in Holland while on a non-cycling trip to the bulb fields with my wife and daughters in the early 1980s. It was used some years later in a feature I contributed to *Cycling Weekly* advocating the development of cycle ways in this country. In the picture we see the typical machine favoured by the Dutch. Holland is a country firmly wedded to the use of the bicycle and, other than for racing cyclists, the machine most in favour is the heavy roadster pictured here, equipped with dynamo lighting, enclosed chain, hub gears and very often hub brakes also, and a substantial carrier used not only for luggage but on occasion for people as well!

The young men seen riding on the cycle path, a ubiquitous feature in Holland, do not scorn to use this type of machine. In fact I can vouch from personal experience that, once under way, they roll steadily and comfortably, their considerable weight being less of a disadvantage in the flat lands of Holland than it might be in hillier terrain.

Driving out early one Sunday morning in 1984 to do my usual coverage of a time trial on one of the Essex courses I overtook Sue Fenwick riding out to compete in the same event. She was one of the leading women riders of the period and presented a most unusual sight as she was carrying her racing wheels on the front of her machine. I got well ahead and then stopped to photograph her as she passed, as by then most racing folk drove out to events by car with their bicycles aboard already equipped for racing. However, from the 1920s to the 1950s, when few people owned cars, it was a familiar sight at weekends as groups of racing men and women cycled out into the countryside on Saturday afternoons on their medium-weight touring wheels, carrying their precious tubular-shod sprint wheels in just the manner shown here. After a night spent in a convivial (and usually cheap!) bed-and-breakfast venue, or perhaps at a club hut, the wheels would be swapped for the Sunday morning competition, and afterwards changed back again for a companionable ride home, usually via lunch stop and tea stop, and very often for an evening inquest on the day's event in the pub before travelling homeward. Although it has bestowed undoubted benefits in some directions the motor car has certainly destroyed valuable aspects of social life.

The wheels are carried here in the time-honoured manner with brackets slotted on to the front wheel spindle and a pair of toe straps used to lash the rims to the handlebars. The brackets, known as sprint carriers, were available from all lightweight cycle dealers but many riders made their own out of strip metal or even utilised old spanners.

Sue seems to have left home before dawn as she has a large front lamp carried on a clip-on handlebar bracket. This is one of the battery-powered products of the Ever-Ready Company who for many years produced a wide range of battery lighting equipment for both cycling and non-cycling purposes. Their cycle lamps could produce very good illumination when new but were susceptible to the inevitable vibration received from the bicycle and quickly became unreliable. It was quite usual to have to pack the lamp with cardboard or similar material to ensure that the battery maintained proper electrical contact.

In the early 1980s there was an upsurge in interest in what came to be termed Human-Powered vehicles, HPVs, as distinct from the plain, unadorned bicycle. These appeared in an infinite variety of forms, mostly concerned with lowering wind resistance, long recognised as the cyclist's worst enemy. Many were based around the recumbent form as typified by the Velocar some fifty years earlier, some employing fairings and enclosures to a varying extent. However, as a result of commercially-sponsored competitions, more and more enthusiasts went for total enclosure, some around recumbent machines, others around more upright positioning.

All this was nothing new, of course. As early as 1913 two Continental speedmen, Oscar Egg of Switzerland and Marcel Berthet of France, had experimented with streamlining and in 1933 Berthet beat the existing hour record set up on a conventional bicycle by over four kilometres. The ride was not recognised officially but Berthet had nevertheless made his point.

My photograph was taken at Woolwich in 1984 in one of the competitions mentioned above, held on closed roads. The machine nearer the camera is something of a compromise, being only partially enclosed, the rider sitting upright and pedalling with legs thrusting forward; very tiring I should think. It appears to be a Continental entry as the rear-view mirror is mounted on the left-hand side. The dents in the fairings would seem to indicate a few mishaps!

The other machine is built around a more or less conventional racing cycle but with disc wheels, just coming into vogue at that time – these are probably overlays on spoked wheels – and the reversed forks and smaller front wheel to bring the fairing as low as possible. This is very similar to the arrangement used by Berthet and Egg all those years earlier. Note the large chainring, indicative of the ability to use higher gears as a result of reduced wind resistance.

The main disadvantage with such machines is that they are difficult to control in side winds and are thus potentially dangerous if used among motor traffic, a problem which has naturally hindered their development commercially.

An example of a completely enclosed HPV is Poppy Flyer, pictured at Herne Hill track during a competition similar to the one I photographed at Woolwich. Constructed by three enthusiasts from Cromer it is of tricycle configuration within a shell of a resin-fibre material similar to that used for boat building. The huge chainring appears to be a TA item, probably to special order at a suitably enormous price, no doubt. The drive is to the small front wheel, hence the need for such a large ring to obtain a high enough gear, while the rear wheels do the steering.

As can be seen, the rider lies flat on his back, pedalling forward and upwards with his head between the rear wheels and when in action the Perspex cover in the foreground is fitted over the rear aperture, enclosing him completely.

The Poppy Flyer proved to be very swift but in this particular design the rider has a very restricted view and it would have no attraction for anyone with the least tendency to claustrophobia. Another problem with these enclosed HPVs is that of ventilation; the human body generates a lot of heat when pedalling and conditions in the 'cockpit' could become rather uncomfortable in hot weather. For this and other reasons already touched upon, machines of this type are unlikely to supplant conventional designs for general use.

Streamlining of a more down-to-earth kind is here demonstrated by Joey McLoughlin as he essays a lone break in a round-the-houses race on closed roads at Rayleigh in 1983. Although he was unsuccessful in this event he went on to win the amateur Tour of Luxemburg later in that season before tuning professional a couple of years later, a move which by and large did not bear the fruit which his earlier career had promised.

As far as the photo itself goes, these head-on shots are very satisfying to capture as one has only the briefest of split seconds to grab the subject as it passes through the point of focus visible in the viewfinder of the SLR. This was before the days of efficient auto focus, and even now I am not sure that its response would be fast enough for a shot such as this. Concentration and anticipation were my watchwords, together with knowledge of the prefocus distance required, about 25 feet with a 135mm lens as here. I am not actually as close as the photo might suggest but I still had to lean back quickly out of the way once the shutter had done its stuff. This and another from the same race were the last pictures of mine to appear in *International Cycle Sport* before it ceased publication shortly afterwards.

I first knew Harold Jones more than sixty years ago when we were both members of the old East London Racing Club. Harold was a talented rider, winner of the Higgins Grand Prix in 1951, but moved away from cycling into motor cycling for a number of years before reviving his interest in the human-powered version by becoming an avid collector of veteran machines. My photograph shows him at a vintage rally at Blackmore, Essex, in the early 1990s. He is demonstrating a machine which can be regarded as the ancestor of modern cycles inasmuch as it represents a type of transport invented around 1760 by a Reigate schoolmaster. It came to be known as the Manumotive Carriage and was the first vehicle to be cycled in the sense that we understand it. This example dates from the mid-19th century, thus predating the first true pedalled cycle, and the influence of the blacksmith and carriage builder in its construction is very evident. Propulsion is by treadle action as employed by Kirkpatrick MacMillan on his two-wheeled Velocipede, and steering is by tiller, both operations requiring considerable effort on the part of the rider.

The booming popularity of family cycling in the first half of the twentieth century posed a need for ways of carrying very young children and manufacturers met this requirement by producing sidecars for attachment to bicycles. They were generally more popular with tandem-riding couples as there were two pairs of legs to cope with the extra weight and drag of the sidecar. However, no matter how carefully fitted there was always a one-sided drag on the steering and it seems strange that no manufacturer, as far as I am aware, came up with a commercially viable trailer. Perhaps there was something psychological in this as the child would have been out of sight of the parent when travelling. Thus it was left to individuals to progress in that direction and in the early 1950s two clubmates of mine built the first examples I can recall seeing, purely for their own use. One was a two-wheeler, quite massively constructed, with a large body suspended in a tubular cradle frame, while the other was carried on a single wheel mounted in swinging arm suspension. Both used a towbar attached by a swivelling joint to the seat cluster. These were eminently successful, much more easily managed than a sidecar, and the youngsters travelled comfortably, yet it was more than twenty years before similar products began to be manufactured commercially on any scale. Paradoxically, it is now extremely rare to see a sidecar in use.

Children grow, of course, and kiddie-seats of one sort or another have long been in use on parents' cycles, either over the rear wheel or attached to the top tube. However, the couple in this photo have equipped their tandem with a most unusual model. Obviously specialist-made in sturdy basketwork it seats the child sideways, which bestows three advantages. Firstly, the youngster is probably kept warmer in cold weather by having both legs tucked snugly together rather than having them divided as in the more usual fore-and-aft position; secondly, there is more room for movement, children can get very bored and uncomfortable in kiddie-seats, particularly at the end of a long day on the road; and thirdly, there is a better view of the passing scene to keep the child amused as less of it is obstructed by the parent's hindquarters.

This was a fortuitous grab shot with a telephoto lens, spotted while in the course of photographing a race, and I doubt if the subjects were even aware that they had been snapped.

The ultimate in child carriage comes from my clubmate Trevor Jones who is carrying baby Laura papoose style in a commercially made harness. This was in the early 1980s and I doubt whether he would have got very far nowadays without some 'health and safety' busybody pouncing on him and putting a stop to what in fact was a perfectly comfortable and satisfactory arrangement for relatively short journeys. At any rate the picture elicited no criticism when it appeared in *Cycling* at the time.

By the early 1990s most of my cycling work centred around time trials in Essex, giving much opportunity for what I might term 'action portraiture'. My subject here is Chris Boardman, still on his way up to world fame, in an early morning shot in damp, dull conditions. So dull in fact that I am using Tri-X film uprated to 800 ISO with the slowest possible shutter speed practicable for this type of action, 1/250 sec, evident in the blurring of the front wheel spokes and also of the background, actually a quite desirable result of the panning process.

Another rider on his way up at the time of this photo was Kevin Dawson, pictured here in 1991 just beginning to show the ability which would take him on to top the BBAR table eleven times, more than anyone else to date. In fact his early challenge, depicted here, was so significant that this particular photo was used twice in a matter of a few weeks in *Cycling Weekly*. It was actually taken with a 100mm lens as I was also shooting in colour with my more usual 135mm lens on the other Chinon SLR.

In 1990 the outcome of both men's and women's Best All-Rounder titles was in doubt until the last weekend of the season when both top contenders were competing in the last qualifying event of the year, the Viking 50 in Essex, both putting in performances that assured them of their respective titles. It was an unusual occurrence to have both BARs going to the last fence, as it were, and I took the opportunity of photographing Gary Dighton and Elaine Ward together, congratulating each other and looking well pleased with the day's ride. Oddly enough this was the only time either of them won the BBAR.

This photograph, taken in the mid-1980s, shows what appears to be a typically modern racing tandem, as indeed it is, except that close examination will show that the riders, Renny Stirling and Vic Haines, are using L-shaped cranks! This product was the biggest confidence trick perpetrated on the cycling world in many a long year as, despite the extravagant claims of its manufacturers, there is no mechanical advantage whatsoever to be gained by having cranks shaped in this way. The turning moment depends entirely on the radius of the circle described by the pedal centres, in this case 170 or 175mm. Nevertheless, numerous riders were gullible enough to spend large sums of money on these cranks although I imagine the two riders here, being top performers of the period, were supplied with theirs for rather less on account of the publicity value. Personally I would be very nervous about the possibility of sudden breakage across the angle of the cranks. I daresay others felt the same as this component disappeared from the market after a year or two.

Otherwise, this tandem is a beautiful machine, the frame being a latterday copy of the Claud Butler Shortbase design, built by Vic Edwards of Romford under his own Rondinella marque. Like many another frame builder he also made frames for other cycle dealers for marketing under their own names.

Ian Cammish was a dominating force in time trialling for over a decade from the start of the 1980s, topping the BBAR table no less than nine times, a record beaten only by Kevin Dawson, depicted elsewhere. Of many photos which I took of Cammish I have selected the one reproduced here as being particularly photogenic, displaying as it does the power and urgency of his riding. 1/500 sec. has stopped the action while the 135mm lens, plus panning, has lifted him out of the background.

Britain's former world champion Mandy Jones is here using the once controversial tri-bars soon after they were permitted in time trial competition in the early 1990s. Tri-bars were invented by competitors in triathlon events in the 1980s with claims that they greatly enhanced performance. However, 'pure' racing cyclists were not allowed to use them for several years but eventually the controlling body bowed to pressure and they were permitted in time trials but not in races from a bunched start.

A primary feature is the elbow rest which, it was claimed, allowed a rider to adopt a less wind resistant position, at the same time placing less load on the back. Certainly, performances have improved steadily since their introduction but whether this is due to the tri-bar itself, the natural spur of competition, increased traffic flows or any other factor is nigh on impossible to determine.

My photo shows Mandy moving from the all-out tri-bar position to a conventional braking position as she approaches a corner. Her machine is an alloy-framed road iron fitted with carbon-fibre wheels. Like tri-bars, disc wheels as on the rear, were an introduction of the late 1980s and initially not permitted in races. Rider pressure triumphed, though, and they became popular with time triallists as it was claimed that although, heavier than spoked wheels, they have an advantageous flywheel effect on courses that are not too hilly. On the debit side, they emit a noisy rumble and are vulnerable to the effect of side winds.

Featured elsewhere but shown here in action is Glenn Longland, riding a bicycle of minimal proportions, seemingly almost too small for him. However, Glenn was experienced enough know what suited him when I took this photo during a time trial in the early 1990s. During a long career he was able to turn his abilities to most branches of the sport but his greatest achievements were against the watch, several national titles falling to his speed legs, but perhaps the greatest prize of all came in 1991 when he became the first rider to top 300 miles in a 12-hour time trial.

In this picture I indulged my penchant for 'figures-in-a-landscape' images when I came across Forty Plus CC members Eddie and Eve Engel at Hadham Ford in Hertfordshire around 1990 and got them to pose for me. I had known them both for many years as Eddie was a regular timekeeper at time trials on Essex courses and Eve was always a vociferous roadside supporter for all and sundry whether she knew them personally or not.

The original of this shot was on 120 colour transparency roll film and it was used as a spread in a feature I wrote for *Saga Magazine* a few years later extolling the virtues of cycle touring and club riding for older folk.

This shot appeared in *Cycling Weekly* in the late Eighties over an editorial feature posing the question "Has the fun gone out of racing?" something I have asked myself more than once in latter years. Certainly this particular event, a Boxing Day time trial on the famous 32nd course in Essex was not generally taken too seriously, many of the entrants riding in fancy dress. The picture shows three Forty Plus members, Eve Engel again, Charlie Merrett at the left and Ken Grant holding up the rider awaiting the timekeeper's "Go!" That rider is none other than Vic Gibbons, British Best All-Rounder in 1953 and 1954, who made a determined comeback late in life and at age sixty was going faster than ever. Some years before this picture I had done an interview feature on Vic and his comeback for *Bicycle Magazine* and in answer to an enquiry he confessed that he had never had any time for touring, preferring to do fast training rides on main roads and that he had little interest in anything other than cycle racing. That may have been the reason why, some years later, as he found his powers waning with age, he took his own life.

Nevertheless, he is obviously enjoying the prospect of a hard winter ride here at the age of around sixty five, well protected against the frost, as I grabbed this picture with the 135mm lens while in the process of photographing finishers on the other side of the road. The short telephoto has pulled the group nicely out of the background here.

Very much involved with Forty Plus CC activities during the early 1990s I went several times to France with them to ride the annual series of *randonnées* based on Boulogne. Run in early September these gave a choice of distances around the Boulonné, that delightful yet comparatively unknown area of hills and woods which lies inland from Boulogne. *Randonnée* is French for what we call a tourist trial and the promotion always attracted a strong entry from Britain. My first picture shows the town square at Samer, the first checkpoint and elevenses halt. Nearly all the riders here are British, doing their bit for the local economy. This picture appeared with a story I did for the short-lived *CycleNews*.

My second picture is of Forty Plus member Bill Turner, photographed at the finish with his award for the oldest rider to finish at the age of eighty and receiving a congratulatory kiss from fellow Forty Plus member Linda Prosser.

My final picture is from the BLRC reunion at Parwich in the Peak District in 1992. The people here are Harold Jones, East London RC, Ray Stevens, Polhill RC, Harry Burvill, East London RC and Paris Cycles independent team, and George Kessock, Polhill RC and Paris Cycles, winner of the 1947 Brighton to Glasgow. All these riders were names to conjure with in my earliest days with the League and I continued in touch with my two East London clubmates on and off for most of my life. 'Burv', like me, was a Forty Plus member in later years and we had much happy riding together until his tragic death in 1999 from Parkinson's disease. The memory lingers on, though, it has been a good life in the cycling world and I am lucky to be able to relive much of it through photographs such as the small selection reproduced herein.